ECONOMICS AND EUROPEAN UNION MIGRATION POLICY

Edited by
Dan Corry

Acknowledgements

This book is based on the main papers given at a Conference held in March 1996 at IPPR in London. This Conference was organised in conjunction with the London office of the Friedrich Ebert Stiftung. Financial support also came from the Lyndhurst Trust for which we are very grateful. Support for the costs of the publication came from the European Commission.

The main work in putting the Conference together was done by Randi Hawkins and the day was run by Glenis Inskip. We are particularly grateful for help in setting things up to Sarah Spencer, Director of the Human Rights Programme at IPPR; to Peter Brannen of the ILO in London; and to Sheila Page of the ODI. The participants at the Conference made very helpful comments on the papers many of which are reflected in the revised texts.

We hope that this volume adds to the knowledge and thinking of people in the UK and the EU on migration and the insights that economic analysis can give into future policy for the EU.

The views expressed in this report are those of the contributors, not necessarily those of the IPPR staff or trustees.

Dan Corry
Senior Economist, IPPR

Contributors

Stuart Bell MP is the Member of Parliament for Middlesborough. He is a member of the Labour Party's Trade and Industry team.

Dan Corry is Senior Economist at the Institute for Public Policy Research in London and editor of its economic policy journal, *New Economy*.

Peter A Fischer and **Thomas Straubhaar** are at the Institute for Economic Policy Research, University of the Bundeswehr, Hamburg, Germany. These authors gratefully acknowledge research assistance and helpful comments by Achim Wolter and Tim Oliver Heinzmann.

Donatella Giubilaro works at the Migration for Employment Branch of the ILO in Geneva

Elmar Hönekopp is at the Institute for Employment Research (IAB) of the Federal Employment Services in Nuremburg

Willem Molle is President of the Board of Directors of the Netherlands Economic Institute (NEI), Rotterdam and Jean Monnet Professor at Erasmus University, Rotterdam

John Salt is at the Migration Research Unit, Department of Geography, University College London

Contents

1. Introduction
   Dan Corry   1

2. The politics of trade and migration
   Stuart Bell MP   7

3. Is Migration into EU-countries demand based?
   Peter A Fischer and Thomas Straubhaar   11

4. The contribution of international aid to the long-term
   solution of the European migration problem
   Willem Molle   50

5. Economic developments within the EU:
   the role of population movements
   John Salt   76

6. Old and new labour migration to
   Germany from Eastern Europe
   Elmar Hönekopp   93

7. European Migration with respect to the
   Maghreb and Turkey: the social and policy challenge
   Donatella Giubilaro   124

1. Introduction
Dan Corry

Who cares about EU immigration?

Why should anyone in the UK care about migration into the EU? After all the modern fears are of large immigration from eastern and central Europe, as well as Turkey, into Germany, and of big movements of people from the Maghreb into Italy, France and Spain. These places are a long way from our shores and are hardly likely to affect us. If we want to talk about immigration, lets talk about the UK's specific points of concern.

This is a natural view. But it is short sighted. In a simple sense, the UK must take a view because it has a vote in the EU. More importantly, the dynamics of migration into the EU and the pressures that even the expectation of migration can engender, have potentially enormous consequences for the political and policy development of the EU and its member nations, and hence for the UK. For those of us from the centre-left, the horrors of inappropriate EU responses to the situation, leading to the rise of intolerance and extreme right wing policies, must be of grave concern. That is why we brought together a Conference and this publication, to discuss these issues, to raise them up the political agenda and to make busy UK policy makers and politicians think about the issues at least for a bit.

Why economics matters for migration policy

But why focus on the economic policy aspects of migration? Surely this is not the core of the issue. But this kind of argument means that economics too rarely gets a look in.

The issue of migration is one that seems to have the potential to get the British public – or at least the tabloid papers that most of them read – in a lather. Any mention of immigration trends, illegal immigrants, or asylum seekers is instantly turned into horrific stories of benefit scroungers, job-snatchers and social problems. In such circumstances, it is hard to have a rational debate and the concept of applying sensible economic analysis to the issues goes out of the window.

Life is often not much better when the concerned economist speaks to the liberal "caring" lobby. In this milieu, it is often stated that only human rights should guide our policy. To talk of economics, is, by many, seen as dangerously instrumental.

Of course it is true that our attitude to our fellow human beings is the mark of how decent we ourselves are. A concern for human rights therefore must take priority over all other things as we consider migration issues. IPPR, under the leadership of Sarah Spencer, has done a great deal of important work in this area, as well as on the issue of forced migration.[1] However, and as her work has recognised, economics has something to add to the debate on migration policy.

On the one hand, there is an important, but too often ignored literature, that shows the economic benefits to the receiving countries from immigration (see eg *Immigration as an Economic Asset* (*op cit*) and Chapter 3 in this volume). Nevertheless, and although we might wish it otherwise, economic policy decisions are often made with at least a half eye on the implications on migration, and in particular for slowing down rates of immigration. This is even more so when we come to external policy, like trade liberalisation and trade policy.

At very least then, we can see what economic theory and applied research can show us about how best to operate these economic policies to reduce migratory pressures, and how to ensure that the benefits that immigration can bring are actually realised. That, in essence, is what this volume is all about.

Markets and migration

The major message from an economic analysis of migration is a ringing shout that migration is good. It is likely to be good for the receiving country and for the sender.

Of course this conclusion is subject to hundreds of qualifications. In a world where markets work perfectly, only those who add something to a country, and can contribute more to the overall wealth of the world by migrating to a country come to it, and all is for the good. It is important to put this view strongly, for too often people start with the dismal approach that migration is simply a bad thing. This is one of the excellent jobs done by Fisher and Straubhaar.

However in the real world, markets are never perfect. Many of the factors that make this so should be tackled as those authors suggest. But some are consequences of things we want for other reasons, both in receiving and sending nations; things like social security, some job protection, and minimum wages. This means we are in what economists call a "second best" world. In such a situation, policies to free the market further, that look theoretically desirable, may reduce economic welfare. In addition, while migration ought to increase the overall level of income in the world, it raises distributional issues. The sending country loses talent and money as well as people; workers who are close substitutes for immigrant workers can lose out and so on. The fact that theoretically the gains from migration could be used to compensate all the losers and still leave the world better off, may not be a very helpful bit of theory.

Nevertheless, the idea that free movement of labour is a good thing, and that immigration can make a positive contribution to economic welfare, is one of the most helpful messages that economics can bring to the party. The idea that as near as perfect mobility of capital and goods as possible must be good has largely been accepted across the political spectrum. The idea that free movement of people is good, which should be a left rallying cry, has yet to take hold.

Push and pull

However, the fact that less barriers to movements are theoretically better than more does not mean we want mass migrations for these can be destabilising all round. Certainly, as Fisher and Straubhaar argue, the first best policy to reduce migration flows is to introduce some kind of action which is non-discriminatory. However, whether their view that this might be a tax applied to all migrants is really such an action, given its effect on those with lower incomes, is arguable.[2] In reality migration flows are regulated by bureaucratic not economic instruments. Nevertheless, one aim should be to ensure that these are as non-discriminatory as possible.

One thing that emerges from the economic analysis is that mass migrations into the EU are probably unlikely, at least on economic grounds. Actual migration flows are, in general, a response to demand for the labour in the receiving country (the pull factor) rather than the state of the labour market in the sending countries (the push factor). The pull factor is dominant partly because if there are no jobs to come to the expected income from immigration goes down and so the incentives to move become less, and also because when there is low demand, countries tend to tighten immigration rules, and historically have been pretty successful. This is one of the reasons that no serious analysis has yet discovered a link between the scale of immigration and the scale of domestic non-employment.

In the case of Germany for instance, as Fischer and Straubhaar illustrate, it is generally the case that when German unemployment is high, immigration from outside the EU goes down (although this is not to deny an upward secular trend in migration to Germany at present, for well-understood reasons). There is little evidence for instance that the rate of migration from Turkey to Germany is very sensitive to Turkish unemployment rates.

To some extent the very hands-on approach to managing immigration flows, as explored in the chapter by Elmar Hönekopp, makes Germany rather different from many other EU countries. In addition, there are some fears that migratory pressure from the Maghreb will in time end the dominance of pull factors. Nevertheless, the experience to date does suggest that pull is more important than push in determining actual flows within the EU.

At present there is not much demand for labour in the EU. Unemployment in the EU is high and the demand for unskilled labour is low and likely to remain so given the changing nature of trade and production as a consequence of globalisation and technological advance. While the regulated nature of many EU labour markets may still create a demand for migrant workers willing to take poor wages and conditions, this is not likely to be a growing market, not least because continental Europe is at least to an extent easing some regulations, cutting back on the generosity of social security benefits and reducing non-wage labour costs.

The story on highly skilled migration is quite different. This often comes from other developed countries, and is something that the EU needs. Indeed ability to attract it becomes a key to competitive advantage as John Salt discusses. Therefore migration polices – both economic and bureaucratic must take this into account.

Reducing migratory pressure

The fact that demand factors dominate actual flows, does not alter the fact that there are many who would like to migrate if the demand and possibility was there. For policy to be successful in reducing the potential for excessive movements of labour, we want to reduce this migratory pressure. How can we do this?

Economic analysis suggests that in the long run, economic growth is the only answer. It is a slow process but not an impossible one. After all countries like Spain and Italy were until relatively recently senders and have now become net receivers of migrants. The process of economic development is difficult and there is the problem, noted by Willem Molle, that the first response to rising living standards and a better educated population, is for the most skilled to emigrate! Nevertheless, economic growth must be our goal.

The secret of economic success remains elusive. Much will be up to the individual countries themselves. But what can the EU do to help?

The first thing, warmly embraced by Stuart Bell, is to open up trade. Such measures, perhaps mediated with clauses to prevent abuse of workers, is by far the most powerful weapon at our disposal. The Euro-Mediterranean agreements, discussed by Donatella Giubilaro, are a major step in the right direction in this area and should be encouraged.[3]

The second thing, is to use overseas aid intelligently. As William Molle emphasises, the aim must be to promote the factors that help spur economic growth. One may disagree with all of his ideas, but the things he focuses on are clearly correct: the key areas are the labour market, education, and good governance as well as making the market work efficiently.

The left position

Much of the economic analysis and economic policy prescriptions presented here may appear somewhat free market and perhaps to some may seem strange in a book emanating from a centre-left organisation. Migration is one of those areas however, where the call for excessive regulation and control is too often a disguised call for racial discrimination and for keeping out foreigners, with no real desire to focus on economic efficiency or social cohesion. To some degree at least, the libertarians and the left can join hands in this area.

We need to make the public aware of the potential benefits of migration, and so counter the natural concerns the public have about it. As the European Commission had put it: "immigration has been a positive process which has brought economic and broader cultural benefits both to the host countries and the immigrants themselves. [Nevertheless] ...anti-democratic elements have sought to exploit the immigration issue. To counter the dangers this poses, governments need to build on the public's tradition of tolerance by putting more energetic emphasis on the benefits of immigration, both economic and social".[4]

We also need research to ensure that whatever controls we do use do not exclude the wrong people. From the highly visible recent case in the UK, where an internationally renowned footballer struggled to get a visa to play in the UK, to the more hidden cases where much needed doctors and other skilled people that we need are excluded, we can begin to see that often the rules turn out to be in nobody's interest at all.[5]

The key thing is to react positively to the migration issue, to seek the benefits available to all, to open ones market, as well as ones heart, to developing countries and to help make policy that helps us all.

Migration policy will always be heavily politically charged. We cannot expect policy makers to act on the best of theory and ideals at all times. But we have a duty to remind them of the facts and of what we know about the truth on migration. We hope this book will play a role in this task.

Endnotes

1 See for example *Strangers and Citizens* ed S Spencer, IPPR, 1994 and *Immigration as an Economic Asset: the German experience*, (Ed. Sarah Spencer) IPPR/Trentham Books 1994

2 Another related proposal suggests using an overall quota that does not discriminate by type of labour so that employers can chose – the argument then being that if they want a foreign worker, it must be because there is a shortage locally in terms of skills and/or price.

3 One should note however that some believe that if the EU was really serious about reducing migratory pressure, it would do something about the massive foreign debt burden that these countries labour under.

4 "On Immigration and Asylum Policies", Communication from the Commission to the Council and the European Parliament, COM (94), Brussels, 1994

5 As *The Economist* recently put it, commenting on British policy towards immigration: "The government's economics are as small-minded as its morality. It looks at those applying to come to work in Britain as a threat, not as a resource". ("Fear of foreigners" 4.5.96)

2. The Politics of Trade and Migration
Stuart Bell MP

The issue of migration into the EU is one that greatly concerns many policy makers. It has the potential to destabilise the economies and societies and even the politics of the EU nations. But, handled correctly, migration offers benefits in all these areas. That is why these issues are so important and I welcome the analysis presented here as to thinking through ways of using economic policy to help shape EU migration policy.

It is an issue that Labour takes very seriously and will continue to do so in government, both in setting its own policies and in joining with our EU partners in shaping a coherent EU policy.

I want to focus on the issue of trade liberalisation and migration, since the two are so intertwined. The key question has to be, will trade liberalisation change migratory patterns?

Trade and New Labour

First of all we need to be clear on our views on trade. New Labour believes trade should be fair and balanced. This goal should be met through the European Union and through institutions such as the World Trade Organisation, the successor to GATT from 1 January 1996. The World Trade Organisation has a key role to play in managing fair trade and in ensuring that regional co-operation through customs unions or other regulatory and economic frameworks is in accordance with WTO rules.

While there is no question that Labour believes that economic growth in the world must be encouraged, this economic growth must go hand in hand with human development. While it is right that the purpose of the WTO is to extend and strengthen the rule of law in international trade, it is of some concern that the Uruguay Round made no provision for workers' rights, with only a reference that this should be part of a working programme for the new WTO.

The whole essence of GATT was that nation states would recognise that in their trade relationships and economic endeavours there would be a quest to raise living standards, thus ensuring full employment built upon the development of the world's resources by expanding the production and exchange of goods.

A social clause within the WTO would outlaw unfair labour practices without in any way legitimising trade barriers against countries which fail to observe these essential conditions. But a social chapter accepted as part of the WTO would enable the new trade body to establish a list of basic labour rights and monitor their application.

The WTO could set up an advisory body that would systematically review the extent to which the WTO parties are meeting their obligations and would deal with complaints of violations to the chapter. The advisory body would be required to recommend to the WTO action for governments to take within a specified time if complaints are upheld by WTO. Trade sanctions could be applied against a country but only if after a period of two years or so it had failed to make adequate efforts to give effect to the recommendations of the advisory body supported by the WTO.

Workers' rights go hand in hand with increased quality of life. We can see too that increased trade does indeed lead to higher living standards.

There has never been a better moment to write a social clause into world trade through the enhanced mechanisms of the WTO, a social clause that would promote basic human rights in employment, rights which should be guaranteed in all countries, and with mechanisms to advance development.

We are also looking at aid to third world countries, looking to see how it might reverse the decline in UK aid spending. New Labour also intends to endorse the United Nations social summit proposal, the so-called 20/20 compact which commits donors to allocating 20 per cent of their overseas development aid, and developing country governments 20 per cent of public expenditure, to basic needs.

EU attitudes to migration

In relation to trade liberalisation and migratory patterns, the European Union has to face up to the issues. Is it prepared to continue being a bastion of wealthy nations facing out to an impoverished third world and seeking to reduce that impoverishment only by aid – that goes to governments rather than their people directly? Or, through trade liberalisation, can the

Union make it easier to import from developing countries, increase the export revenues of the poorer states, so creating employment in these countries and alleviating the need to migrate? To me it is clear that the latter strategy – in addition to aid – is vital.

Poorer countries themselves, however, have to wish to participate in this process. The truth is that many poorer countries do not mind migration of their population to wealthier countries, given the receipts they receive when foreign currency is returned to their country by those who have left their families behind. The challenge is therefore two fold: the challenge to the European Union to provide more opportunities for imports from poorer countries; and the desire of poorer countries to halt the migration of their own populations.

Trade liberalisation offers a double benefit; the Union would be stronger and so too would be the poorer countries. The EU would have more choice of goods in their own consumer societies, and the poorer countries would have the wealth upon which to build their own economies for the benefit of their peoples.

A Euro-Mediterranean partnership is one route forward with respect to many of the sending countries, covering all forms of action falling under the Treaty of Rome and the amendments leading to the European Union. The establishment of a Euro-Mediterranean Economic Area is part of, and should go hand in hand with, the creation of an area of peace and stability.

Such an Economic Area should involve not only free trade arrangements but also a range of measures on the part of the Union to help the poorer countries of the Area to modernise their economies in the interests of sustainable development, preserving at the same time their equilibrium and their identity.

A long journey

The journey of a thousand miles, as we all know, begins with a single step, but we can see too the difficulties that will continue if we are unable to tackle trade liberalisation on the one hand and migration on the other, a tangled web of strands that are political, economic and which can give rise to political unrest and injustice.

The issues are complex and difficult in a world where there is global competition for scarce resources and for access to foreign markets, competition between individuals in the labour markets, and an often tense relationship between capital and labour.

Inward investment can make the difference between employment and unemployment; the decision of a multi-national to locate in a particular country can make the difference between staying in that country or moving on in search of a better standard of living. But of course the greatest disadvantage of migration is that countries may lose some of their best educated and enterprising people, their highly skilled workers.

The challenge therefore is to encourage these people to stay in their own countries and to contribute to the economic and social development of these countries.

It is for these reasons that we shall need to work through all the agencies and regional groupings we can to create the frameworks of full, fair and managed trade for countries to have the will to keep their people at home, to build social progress into their domestic agendas, and to accept that all this will take many years. The EU has a particularly important role here. We must work to see whether our policies can be better co-ordinated to help solve these gigantic issues of our time – in a spirit of optimism and co-operation and not in a negative, defensive way. The work of the WTO and the United Nations is also very important.

There are many difficult decisions to be made. But we need to get on and take the first steps together.

3. Is Migration into EU countries demand based?
by Peter A Fischer and Thomas Straubhaar

Introduction

For some time now, migration has been a highly controversial issue in public debate and it has reached the top of the political agenda in many European countries, as well as in Northern America. But the usual content of discussion and envisaged action is of a strikingly defensive nature. There seems to be a fear that the economically highly developed European societies could become overwhelmed by mass immigration from the poorer South and the East and that things may get "out of control". Migration is perceived as something that threatens living standards and welfare. Henceforth, public debates often conclude that "something has to be done".

This paper argues that most of the fears concerning migration lack clear justification once they are confronted with the implications of migration theory as well as with empirical evidence. Most people are geographically and culturally immobile and wish to remain so. Out of those few who would really like to migrate into the EU, most will be unable to do so, because they are not economically "wanted". They therefore lack the means to move and they cannot make a sufficient living within an EU country. The overall trend is slowing population growth and ageing populations with important economic consequences in western and central Europe. Irrespective of present unemployment problems this will in the medium term create a vacuum in the labour markets of the European Economic Area (EEA) and hence immigration demand.[1] Migration and labour mobility are an essential ingredient of economic integration and correspond to the key economic logic of the European Common Market. Migration is economically efficient and beneficial, provided we allow economic incentives to determine it. Reaping the benefits of economic integration is likely to require at least some degree of labour mobility. The development of welfare societies and the spread of dual career households, however, make people increasingly immobile. The ability to attract scarce mobile labour is therefore likely to become a key-element of locational competition within countries. With respect to the "wanted", migration will become a quest rather than a threat.

There is, however, a need for "something to be done", namely the explicit formulation of a more innovative, forward-looking common European migration policy for at least three reasons: (a) in order to be economically beneficial, (im)migration and occupational choices of foreigners have to be determined by economic incentives. This requires a migration policy that allows market mechanisms to work as far as possible. (b) Even though migration is generally perceived as economically efficient, it invokes distributional consequences that create "winners" and "losers" and may change the structure of a society in a socially undesired way. For this trade-off, a regime of completely free migration is unlikely to be a feasible policy option in the near future. Migration from outside the EU will continue to be restricted. But we are going to demonstrate that the restriction of immigration from non EU-countries requires the design of a common European migration policy. (c) Political and ecological reasons are likely to increase forced migration. Resulting requests for admission are difficult to neglect purely on the grounds of lacking economic demand. It has to be realised, though, that the welcoming of people for humanitarian and ethical reasons is often more costly and less efficient than to take joint action in order to prevent the root causes of forced migration. (d) There is, unfortunately, little prospect of a fast convergence between the developed and the less developed world. The number of disadvantaged people in the South and East who dream of moving for a better living but lack the opportunity to do so (because they are not "wanted" economically anywhere in the North) is bound to increase. This creates at least moral arguments for trying to reduce the migration potential out of the South and East.

While reasons (a) and (b) demonstrate the need for an internal migration policy including rules on entry and exit and action to be taken in order to remove remaining obstacles to free mobility within the European economic area, reasons (c) and (d) require the design of an external migration policy in order to reduce the migration potential in the South and East. Both elements of such a migration policy, the "domestic" as well as the "foreign" part, are inefficient if the basic rules are not common for all the EU countries. Once this is recognised, however, migration ceases to appear as a threat, requiring defensive action. It rather becomes a challenge for innovative and visionary policy making.

The paper is organised as follows: the next section discusses who would like to come and who is likely to be wanted from the point of view of (economic) migration theory as well as with respect to some recent empirical evidence on migration within and into the EU. It concludes with a brief investigation of the degree that demand determines migration into the EU. The following section states the need for a migration policy from the economic perspective. We then summarise existing EU regulations in the field of migration and formulates ten guidelines for what needs to be done. Finally we conclude.

Who would like to come, who is likely to be wanted

Push or pull: implications from migration theory
Why do people move? Numerous possible explanations have been set forth to answer this question. Most integrated theoretical answers are essentially advanced formulations of the so called "push-pull approach" pioneered by Lee (1966). According to this well performing theory, migration results from the interaction of (supply side) push factors in the area of emigration and (demand side) pull factors in the area of immigration. Migration occurs only if there are both, sufficient push factors which create the desire to emigrate and pull factors creating a demand for immigration. Furthermore, intervening factors like lacking information, institutional arrangements hampering mobility and political regulations have to be overcome.

These points can best be considered in a multi-disciplinary, push-pull framework. With respect to the causes of migration, we must emphasise what essentially all theories of migration have in common, namely the belief that differences in environmental macro factors of geo-political units (counties, regions, countries, larger areas like common markets) cause migration. The exact form of these differences, however, can vary. We call the analysis of migration-inducing environmental differences between geo-political units the "macro level" of migration research.

Individual human beings, in this terminology the "micro-level" of analysis, compare the macro-level units by looking at the perceived differences between them. These are by no means exclusively economic but include also differences in the cultural, political and geo-ecological situation. People then weigh the different advantages and disadvantages of their present macro-level unit of residence against the potential alternatives and decide whether they want to remain within their present area of residence (decision to "stay") or whether they want to move to a different geo-political unit (decision to "go").

All "go"-decisions by the inhabitants of a macro-level-unit at a given time constitute the migration potential of this unit. Let us assume a world, made up of two countries A and B. All inhabitants of country A who are willing to migrate to B make up A's migration potential at time t. This potential faces B's demand for immigration which is determined by macro factors and willingness of B's inhabitants' to accept immigrants from A. In a situation where B needs and is willing to accept all immigrants from A, B's migration potential could entirely transform into effective migration. Whether and how fast this would happen depends on the presence and magnitude of intervening obstacles like poor or biased information, institutional and legal hindrances or procedural requirements. If the economy in B has no need for migration or if inhabitants of B are not willing to accept immigration from A, actual migration is unlikely to occur and migration potential transforms into what one may call migration pressure (Straubhaar, 1993).

If in this A-B-world, pull factors in A create demand for more migrants than the number of people in B who are willing to move, one will find actual migration to be supply determined. There is evidence that in some fast developing centres of industrialised countries, internal mobility has been essentially supply determined. People could find better paid jobs in industrial centres if only they would like to move there.

But if the number of people who would like to migrate is smaller than the number of those who are wanted, migration becomes demand determined. In this case, which seems to be especially true for the current migration situation of unskilled people in many developing countries, people may desire to go somewhere else, but they lack the means to do so and the opportunities to make a living that would allow them to stay somewhere else. Usually, however, actual migration is simultaneously determined by both, supply and demand factors.

To obtain a more realistic assessment of migration potential, one has to consider what determines people's decision to migrate.

This framework for thinking about migration distinguishes between (a) existential economic needs (b) needs for security (c) needs for social integration and acceptance and (d) needs for self-fulfilment.[2] It looks not only at economic costs and benefits of migration but it takes non-economic factors explicitly into account. After all factors like peace, freedom, security, love, health and happiness, to mention just a few, are very important elements of life and can not be excluded from considerations about the effects of migration.

Economic migration theories have traditionally focused on (a) and (b) in order to explain migration.[3] Reasons (c) and (d) have more often been covered by sociological and psychological theories of migration.[4] Nevertheless, economic theories can help us understand why the large majority of people do not want to move, despite supposed important incentives (Hammar, 1994). In what follows, we will concentrate on economic contributions to migration theory in order to explain the demand and/or supply determination of actual migration flows.

Classical or neo-classical economic theory (Hicks, 1932) has identified income or rather wage differences relative to migration costs as the major determinant of migration. Given the huge differential in wages between the South and East on the one hand and the North on the other hand and given the dramatic decrease in transportation and communication costs, this simple theory would lead us to expect an enormous migration potential. Maybe this is where most common European fears of mass migration emanate from. But subsequent developments in the micro theory of migration have drawn attention to further important variables which have important roles in determining migration potential:

1 *The Harris-Todaro (1970) approach* emphasised that people weigh outcomes at different locations by looking at the expected probabilities of realising each of them. Not only wage level differences and relative costs of movement matter, but also labour market conditions like employment growth and unemployment levels (Herzog, Schlottman and Bohem (1993), Ghatak and Levine (1993)).

2 *The Human-Capital approach* pioneered originally by Sjaastad (1962) and Becker (1964) stresses that comparing macro-level conditions at a certain point in time cannot explain migration decisions sufficiently because the decision to migrate involves a dynamic assessment: it should therefore be thought of in similar terms to any investment decision. Thus, expectations about the (insecure) future, attitudes towards risk and preferences for the present are important determinants of migration decisions. People who do not care too much about the future may want to avoid the short run costs of migration even if migration promises relatively high benefits in the more distant future.

3 *Search theories* (McCall and McCall, Berninghaus and Seifert) outline why information is a decisive element in determining migration patterns (and eventually sequential migration and job search processes). As migration is not costless, people may find it rational not to consider

migrating at all or to head for "second best solutions". This is why the cheap availability of information about potential migration destinations, for instance due to history or the existence of 'migration networks' (Massey *et al*, 1993), is often the key-explanation for the direction of actual moves.

4 *The "New Economics of Migration"* (Stark, 1991) scrutinises how insights about the creation of migration potential change if we allow the family or a group rather than an independent individual to determine migration decisions. This gives room for insurance and risk considerations (Stark and Bloom, 1985) as well as for accounting for aspects of relative deprivation (Stark and Taylor, 1989) and changes of social status within reference groups.

5 *The value of immobility approach* (see Becker, 1962 and Chiswick, 1986 for a firm-specific and production-side oriented treatment, Fischer, Martin and Straubhaar, 1995a for a more comprehensive approach) emphasises that immobility has a value of its own. To stay at a certain location allows people to accumulate society-, firm- and space-specific 'insider advantages' that are non-transferable and thus lost if migration occurs.

6 *The 'inverted-U curve hypothesis'* (Faini and Venturini, 1994; Fischer, Martin and Straubhaar, 1995b) links the level of economic development or personal wealth with the propensity to migrate. It can be derived from micro-economic considerations about the relative importance of existential and other needs. According to this hypothesis, people who struggle to cover their subsistence needs may be willing to move, but they are unlikely to migrate internationally because they do not have the means to cover initial costs of migration. If the societies they are living in develop economically and if individual welfare increases, more families will be able to cover the initial costs of sending at least one member of the family abroad. The economic development of societies will therefore first increase migration potential. Beyond a certain watershed, however, where subsistence needs become relatively less important and the economic, social and political costs of mobility make it more and more attractive to stay, migration potential will be reduced again. Of course, in times where development deteriorates, the opposite will be true. Faini and Venturini estimate this watershed level at a *per capita* income of around US$4,000; Fischer, Martin and Straubhaar (1995b) come to similar conclusions but point to the fact that the development of mobility propensities ought to be different for short distance (regional)

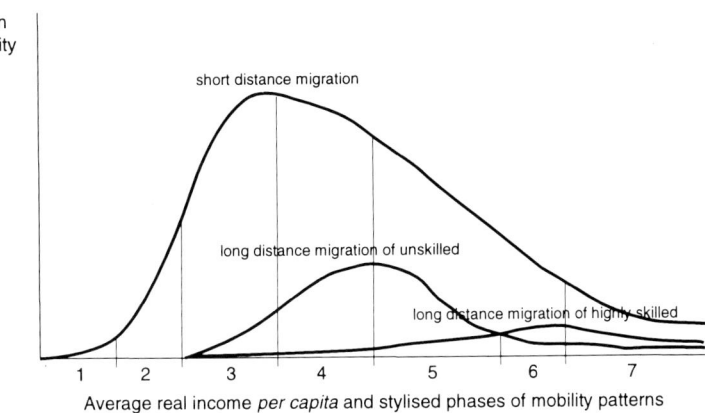

Fig. 3.1: Migration propensity and development: the modified inverted U-curve

migration, long distance (international) migration by the unskilled and for migration of the highly skilled. Fig. 3.1 illustrates this point graphically.

The above enumeration is of course not complete but it allows some theoretical insights about the migration potential and gives some answers to the question of who would like most to migrate into EU-countries. These are not just those who are poorer and therefore expect higher incomes when moving, but:

a *Those who are young* (because their time horizon is longer and their investment in location-specific insider advantages lower) and relatively independent.

b *Those who face a high probability of finding a job* and making a good living in the labour market of the immigration area but do not expect an improvement of their situation at their present location in the near future.

c *Those who have cheap access to information about a certain area.* Therefore, those who desire to come are most likely to be found in geographically not too distant places that have some cultural or historical and/or language links to the prospective immigrant society.

d   *Those whose skills and abilities are relevant and therefore transferable* into the immigrant societies (because of the value of immobility). From an economic point of view, this will be mostly relatively well educated people and people from economies that have reached a level of development and of economic organisation that is not too different from the potential immigrant area. However, people from such societies are not very likely to desire to come, because of point "e".

e   *Those who live in rapidly developing areas of less-developed countries.* Immigrant potential will neither be largest in highly developed nor in the poorest economies. Willingness to migrate over longer distances is most likely to increase in less developed areas that enjoy periods of fast development and transition. Once economies reach a certain level of development (and therefore become more similar to EU-countries), their inhabitants' desire to migrate is bound to decrease. Normally these economies then become net immigrant areas themselves.

But are those who would eventually like to come those who are 'wanted'?
After the second world war, the structural shortage of unskilled labour led European countries to welcome the immigration of unskilled workers who had some cultural or historical links to the immigrant societies. Germany and Switzerland built up so called "guest worker systems" inviting people from Southern economies to help building up the host economies (Fischer and Straubhaar, 1995), Sweden welcomed thousands of Finnish manual workers (Westin, 1994; Fischer and Straubhaar, 1996) and France and Britain accommodated relatively openly members of their (former) colonies (Coleman, 1995; Salt 1995a, 1995b). But with increasing world-wide economic integration, further international specialisation and economic development, the European economies have lost their competitive advantage in labour intensive production, which requires large scale employment of unskilled workers.

As the wealth of European economies increases, the more international labour division emerges where production that requires unskilled work are imported and developed economies specialise in the production and provision of high productivity work that demands correspondingly higher skills (Findlay, 1993; Krugman, 1995; Salt & Singleton, 1995). As some unskilled work, especially in the service sector, is not tradable, a limited need for unskilled work will persist, however. Because these simple jobs are low paid and thus relatively unattractive for natives, some demand for immigration of unskilled is likely to remain. At present, however, unskilled labour in most European countries suffers from particularly high unemployment rates, and with further economic development and structural change continuing, large scale demand for unskilled immigrants is likely to continue to decrease.

With economic integration advancing, the scope for local specialisation and exploitation of scale economies of concentration (Krugman, 1991) increases. Correspondingly, we expect two kinds of people to become more 'wanted' from the point of view of an immigrant area:

- those who are locally non-available (or only at more expensive terms), well educated and/or trained specialists[5]

- those who live in the periphery of newly emerging centres of economic activity, particularly urban agglomerations.

Synthesising this discussion of theoretical insights into who is most likely to migrate into the EU and who will be most "wanted", we conclude that young and relatively well educated people from culturally linked and geographically not too distant areas that undergo periods of relatively fast development or transition are the most likely to move. From this point of view, future integration of the former communist economies in the near East will be most significant for the origin and scale of future migration flows into the EU. After all, not just present wealth differences, but expected prospects for future development matter for migration decisions. In higher developed countries, people usually become more immobile due to the increasing accumulation of a "value of immobility" and due to non-economic needs. In very poor countries, people do not migrate because they do not have the means to cover the initial costs.

The migration potential of unskilled workers is bound to exceed the demand of European labour markets. Unskilled labour migration will therefore be demand determined. Highly skilled specialists however will become more "wanted". Availability of highly skilled specialists could become a key determinant of (regional) economic development. But for micro-economic reasons we do expect the migration propensities of highly skilled individuals to decrease. Migration of highly skilled specialists will henceforth be rather supply determined. Finally, people's willingness to migrate from the periphery into the centre may determine the rise and fall of local centres.[6]

Some empirical evidence on migration in and into the EU and the UK
The World Bank estimates that in 1985, 105.5 million people were on the move or lived outside their country of origin. That represents about two per cent of the total world population. Approximately 20 million or 19 per cent were fleeing political persecution or war (ILO/IOM/UNHCR 1994). The IOM has estimated the global potential of those who would eventually like to come to higher developed areas at about 80 to 100 million people. Thereof, about 60 million would like to move permanently and 20 million temporarily. About 15 million are refugees and asylum seekers and approximately 30 million are illegals (IOM, 1991).

The actual migration into the EU looks rather modest. In 1993, only about 18 million (4.8 per cent) of all citizens in EEA countries were foreigners, ie people of a citizenship other than that of the country they are resident in (Eurostat, 1996).[8] Only 3.3 per cent were citizens from outside the EEA. Net immigration of all foreigners into EEA countries in 1993 equalled less than 0.3 per cent of the total population.

In 1993, the largest absolute size of foreigners in the EU could be found in Germany (6.5 millions), France (3.6 millions), the United Kingdom (2.2 millions) and in Italy (0.9 millions) which has turned from the classical European emigration country into an immigration country. Once we look at the share of foreigners in the total population, however, smaller countries enter into the leading positions. In the EU, Germany (eight per cent) was accompanied by Luxembourg (30 per cent[9]), Belgium (nine per cent) and Austria (6.6 per cent) as the four countries with the highest share of foreign population. In the EEA, all of them were outnumbered by Liechtenstein with 38.3 per cent: due to the dominance of short distance migration, it is not surprising that small countries that share a relatively long borderline with other European countries tend to have higher shares of foreign citizens.

Fig. 3.2 shows the origin of foreigners by citizenship in the four EU countries that hosted the largest numbers of non-nationals. The charts further underline the relatively high share of immigrants from outside the EU. They illustrate impressively the importance of geographical proximity (especially for France), colonial and cultural links (UK and France) and the significance of history and migration networks (Germany).

Is migration into EU countries demand based? 21

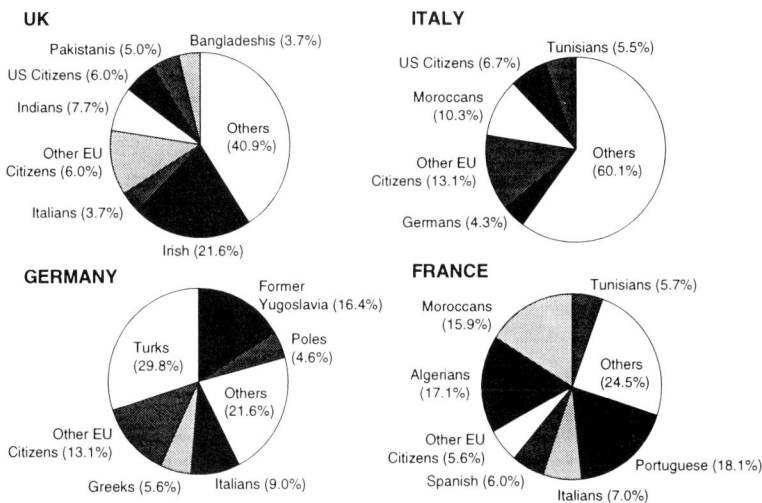

Fig. 3.2: Non-nationals in selected EU countries by citizenship, 1993
Source: Eurostat (1996)

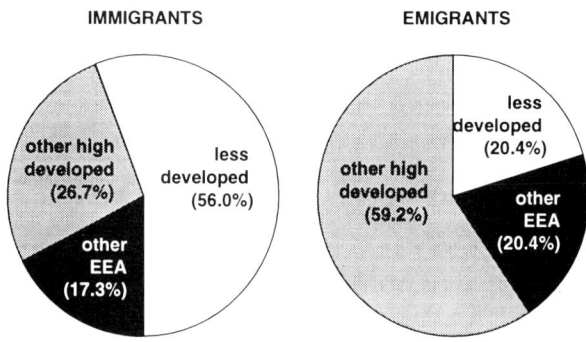

Fig. 3.3: Country of origin of non-national immigrants and emigrants in EEA countries by development level, 1993
Datasource: Eurostat (1996)

With respect to immigration, Fig. 3.3 depicts the composition of immigrants into the EEA in 1993 who were of foreign nationality. Eurostat estimates that in 1993 about one fourth (25.9 per cent) of all who immigrated into EEA countries were nationals (returnees). Out of all non-nationals around one in four was another EEA citizen. Another one in four come from a developed non-EEA country, while the remaining two originated from a less developed country. But as far as emigration is concerned, only one out of five emigrants was a citizen of a low developed country, while three were non-EEA developed country nationals. Thus, while more citizens of low developed countries enter the EU than leave, the net balance is strongly negative with respect to citizens of other developed countries. Though weak, this lends some support for our theoretical hypothesis that people who have reached a certain threshold wealth but originate in low developed countries have higher propensities to migrate into the EU than people from other developed countries.

In most EU countries then, the share of EU immigrants is decreasing while the number of non-EU immigrants is increasing. Though EEA citizens enjoy more or less full freedom of movement, their mobility is decreasing. Even citizens of previously 'classical' immigration countries like Greece, Portugal and Spain have not increasingly migrated to other EU countries after joining the EU. On the contrary, their share in migration flows has fallen since.

For those EU countries where data is available, overall gender distribution of immigrants has been rather balanced; about as many males immigrated to EU countries as females.

Let us have a somewhat closer look at immigration into the UK.[10] Fig. 3.4 shows the share of immigrants to the UK who were born in another EU country. It is fairly minor and has not increased in recent years. As expected, immigrants were on average particularly young (Fig. 3.5). One fourth of all male and even one third of all female immigrants were between 15 and 24 years old; 70 per cent of male immigrants and 76 of female ones were aged 15–44. In 1992, 57 per cent of all immigrants were employed prior to migration.

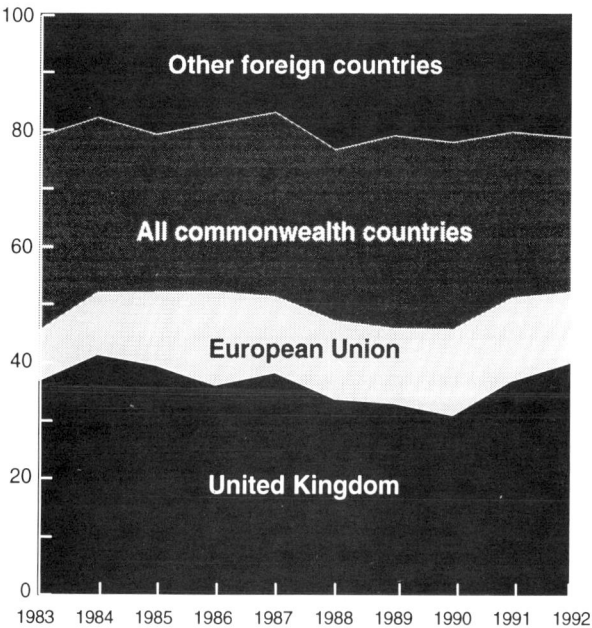

Fig. 3.4: Birthplace of immigrants into the UK, 1983–1992
(% of total immigration)

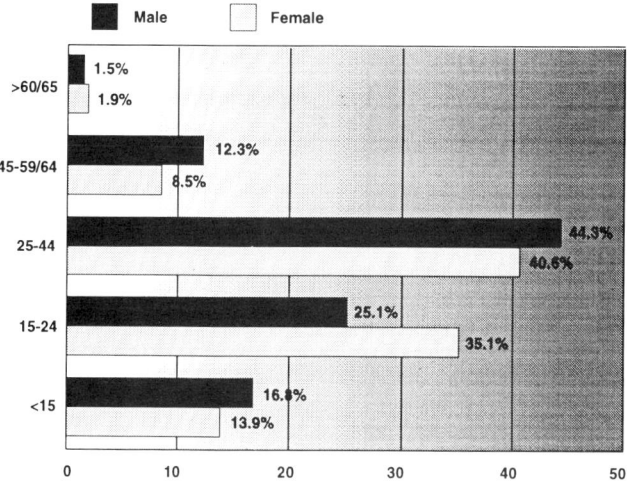

Fig. 3.5: Age and sex distribution of immigrants into the UK 1992

Both figures; Source: HMSO (1995).

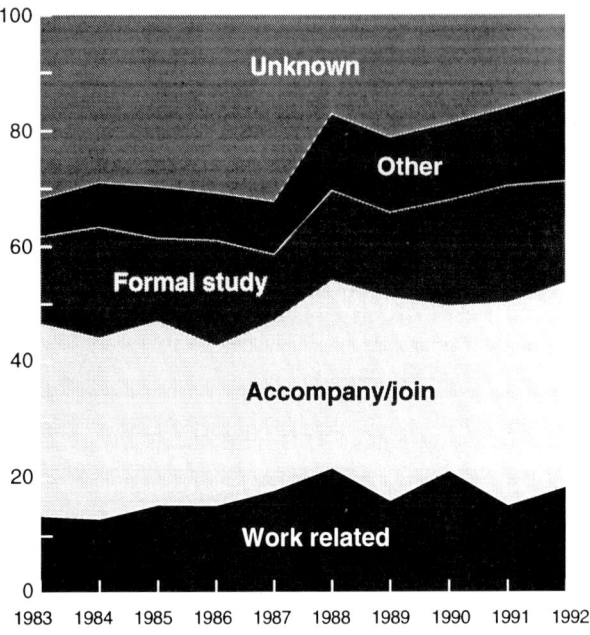

Fig. 3.6: Recorded reasons for immigration into the UK, 1983–1992 % of total immigration

Datasource: HMSO (1995), CSO (1995).

Although the majority of immigrants come from less developed countries, roughly 60 per cent had professional and managerial occupations, 40 per cent did manual and clerical jobs before migrating.[11] The immigrant age group 15–24 was dominated by females. The sex distribution of all other age groups is biased towards men, apart from pensioners where the numbers are about equal (Fig. 3.5).

Fig. 3.6, on reasons for migration into the UK, illustrates another typical feature of today's immigration into EU countries. Only between ten and twenty per cent of all UK immigrants reported having moved for work related reasons. Simultaneously, the share of those who accompany or join an economically motivated migrant (family reunion) is increasing together with those who move for "other reasons". This phenomenon limits the scope for effective migration policy measures aimed at those economically motivated to migrate.

To summarise the empirical evidence on immigration into the EU, we may state that figures for the EEA in general and the UK in particular show that immigrants originate increasingly from outside the EU and particularly from developing areas. For the choice of the host country, historical, cultural and colonial links as well as geographical proximity still play an important role. Especially within the EU, most people move "regionally". Immigrants in the EU are usually young and their gender distribution seems to be balanced overall. In the UK, only between 10 and 20 per cent of them immigrated for work related reasons. More people came to join or accompany somebody or to study. Nevertheless, more than half of those who immigrated into the UK in 1992 were employed prior to immigration and most of them had professional and managerial occupations; only a minority were previously employed in manual and clerical jobs. All in all, the five per cent share of non-nationals now residing within the EU is surprisingly low.

Is migration into EU countries demand based?

We have argued that migration is simultaneously determined by push and pull (supply and demand) factors. For migration from lower developed countries, migration potential is likely to outweigh migration demand. In other words, not all of those who would like to come and stay find an opportunity to do so. In these cases we expect migration to be demand determined. For immigration from highly developed countries, however, supply factors are likely to play a more important role. We take up this point by investigating the determination of migration flows into Germany. The main reason for using Germany as an example is that migration data is usually rather scarce and unreliable even for EU countries but the German case is exceptionally well documented and labour market data is available for the main sending countries too.

Fig. 3.7 (overleaf) depicts annual immigration propensities into Germany (immigration as a percentage of total population; left hand scale) against the development of the West German unemployment rate (seasonally adjusted, right hand scale). At the beginning of the 1960s the immigration propensity of (non-national) migrants from outside the EU was still below that of EU immigrants. During the 1970s and 1980s, immigration from other EU countries remained at the low level of below 0.5 immigrants per 100 inhabitants with a falling trend and little variation. Immigration of non-nationals from outside the EU[12] increased sharply during the last thirty years. At the end of the 1980s, it approached (the relatively low) level of German internal mobility. Although showing similar patterns as intra-EU

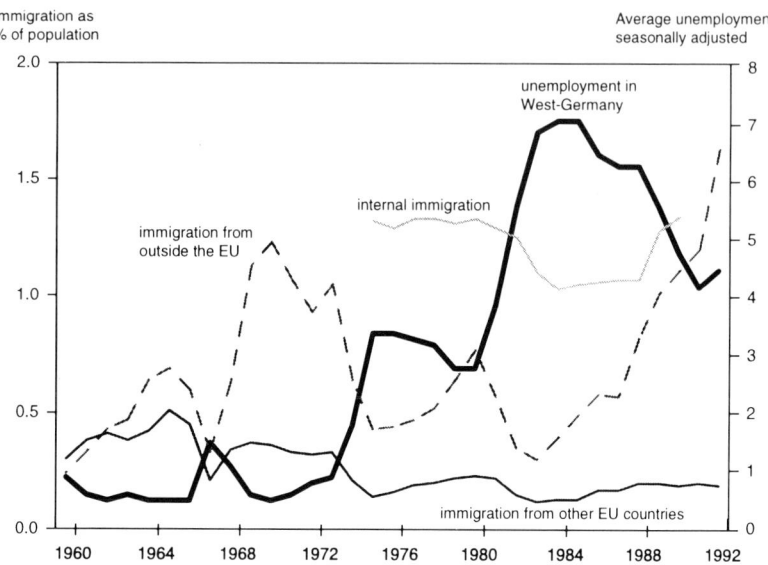

Fig. 3.7: Immigration propensities and unemployment in Germany

Datasource: Eurostat (various editions)

immigration, extra-EU immigration has exhibited much stronger fluctuations then intra EU-flows. We have tested these fluctuations against GDP growth, employment growth and unemployment rates. The most obvious relation is the strongly symmetric behaviour of third-country immigration and unemployment rates shown in Fig. 3.7. A decrease in West-German unemployment rates has been associated with an increase in third-country immigration and increases in unemployment clearly led to decreases of immigration rates. To the extend that unemployment rates are good proxies for (business cycle determined) labour demand, Fig. 3.7 suggests that immigration into Germany has indeed been demand determined, especially as far as immigration from outside the EU is concerned. This third country immigration has also been subject to the obvious trend that took place irrespective of the business cycle.

How about the interplay of pull and push factors? Figs. 3.8a–c depicts immigration into Germany from Italy, Greece and Turkey against GDP, employment and unemployment patterns in the sending and receiving countries. Italy illustrates the case of an economically fast developing EU member country, Greece has been a third country until becoming an EU

Figs. 3.8a–c: Labour market determination of immigration to Germany

See overleaf for figs. b and c
Sources: Eurostat (various editions); Summers and Heston (1994).

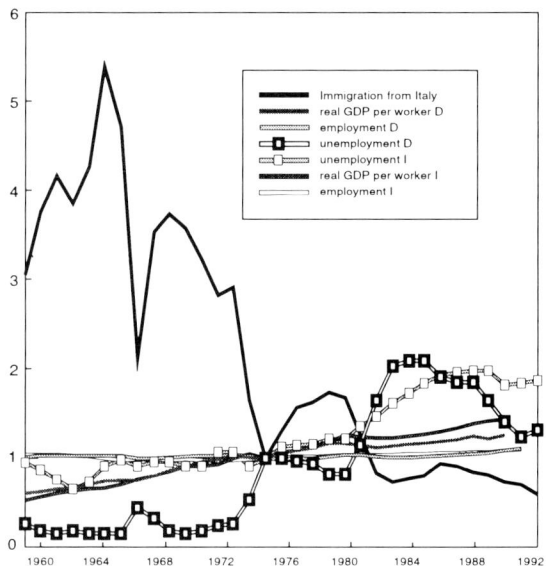

Fig.3.8a: Labour market determination of immigration from Italy: Index; 1975=1

member and Greek labour being finally entitled to free movement within the EU from 1987 onwards. Turkey represents an important and typical third country sending area.[13]

For Italy, the trend of strongly decreasing mobility going along with growth of GDP per worker shows off most clearly. Again, fluctuations are negatively correlated with German unemployment rates, but no clear relation between Italian unemployment rates and migration can be detected. During the 1980s, Italian unemployment increased sharply but migration of Italians into Germany did not react to any serious extent. It seems that Italian immigration

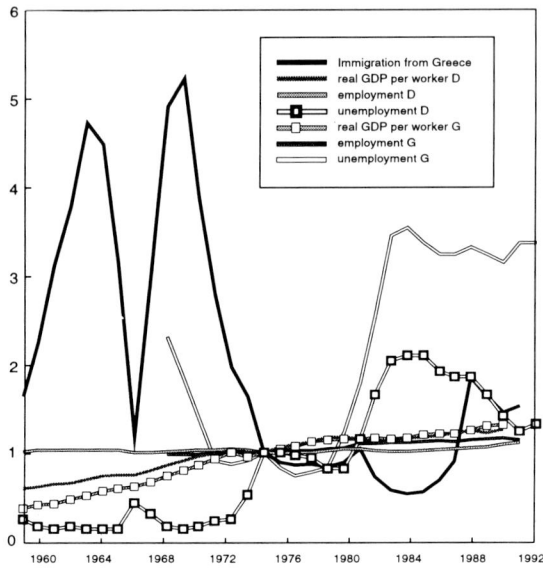

Fig. 3.8b: Labour market determination of immigration from Greece: index; 1975=1

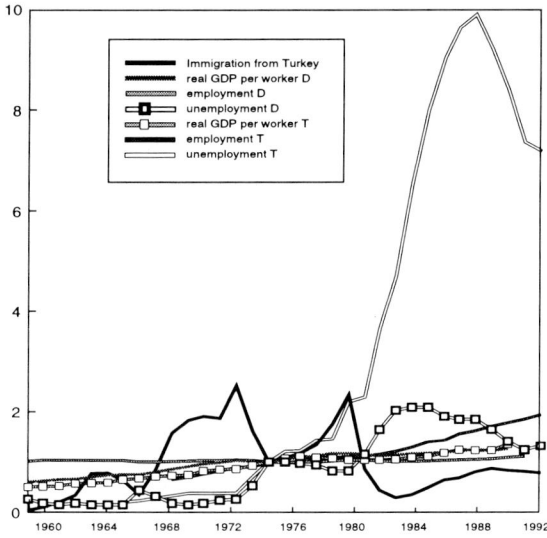

Fig. 3.8c: Labour market determination of immigration from Turkey: index; 1975=1

has been demand determined, but possibly also driven by a strong decrease of migration potential with advances in Italian economic development and convergence towards the economic development of other EU countries.[14]

In the 1960s the immigration of Greeks was up to five times higher than in 1975. Since then it has remained relatively constant at a considerably lower level although Greek unemployment has increased seriously during the eighties. The granting of freedom of movement within the EU resulted in a small increase of Greek emigration in 1988 that was immediately followed by a decrease in 1989 and the following years. Again the data in Fig. 3.8b suggests that immigration from the non-EU country Greece has been largely demand based at least in early years, while the decrease in the number of Greeks who were considering emigrating might have become a more important factor in determining migration flows in recent times.

The strongest evidence for the dominance of pull factors in the determination of migration from outside into the EU comes from Fig. 3.8c. Immigration from Turkey is also clearly symmetric to changes in the West German unemployment rate. Decreases in unemployment were associated with increases in immigration from Turkey and vice versa. But the increase in the Turkish unemployment rate resulted in a (slight) increase in immigration of Turks to Germany only until the labour market situation in Germany started to deteriorate in the 1980s. Then, immigration decreased below 1975 levels despite a tenfold increase in the Turkish unemployment rate between 1975 and 1989: Immigration from Turkey to Germany was clearly demand driven.[15]

Changes over time
The pattern of who would like to come and who is likely to be wanted has changed over the years. Fig. 3.9 (overleaf) shows a stylised comparison of labour demand and supply patterns in north-west Europe in the 1960s and the 1990s, taken from Böhning (1995).

In the 1960s, domestic labour demand was relatively equally spread between high skilled, skilled and low skilled, with the majority being skilled. There were labour market shortages in high skilled and low skilled jobs. As the migration potential in the most important (southern) emigration countries consisted mainly of unskilled workers, there was an important immigration of unskilled and some immigration of high skilled but almost none of (medium) skilled.

a: Western and Northern Europe, 1960s

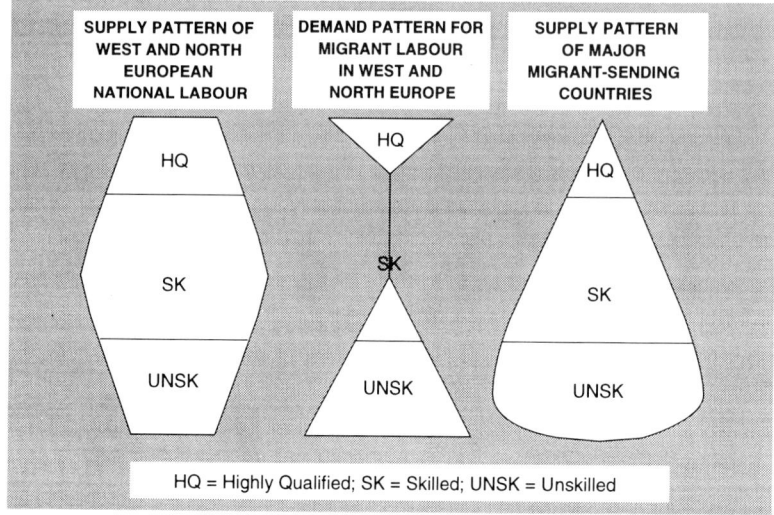

b: Western and Northern Europe, 1990s

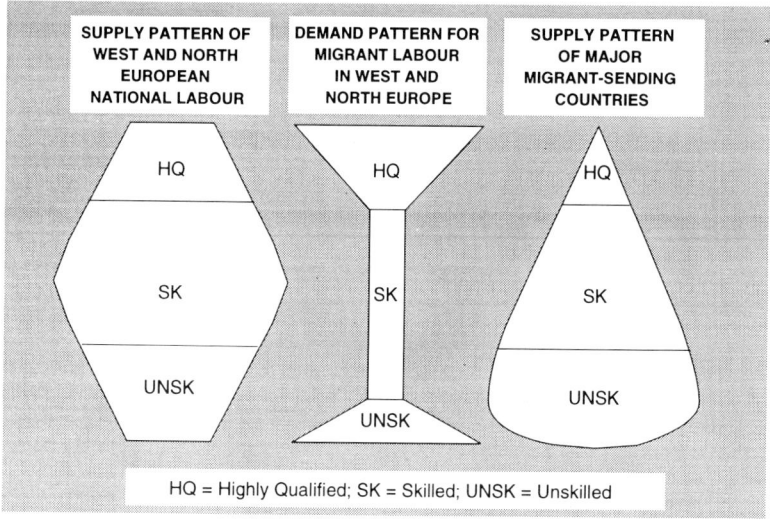

Fig. 3.9: Stylised labour demand and supply patterns and migration demand in the 1960s and 1990s

Source: Böhning (1995)

In the 1990s, educational efforts in the north-western European countries have led to a further relative increase in the provision of domestic skilled labour. North-western countries have a relatively high demand for high skilled foreign labour, little demand for skilled and some demand for low skilled. People within the EU have become increasingly immobile. Immigrants therefore come more and more from outside the EU. As this migration potential consists above all of the unskilled, immigration of unskilled (and medium-skilled) is and will be primarily demand based. In the small scale intra-EU migration, both demand and supply factors will play a role, with supply factors gaining momentum. Although remaining probably fewer in absolute numbers, migration of high skilled specialists is likely to become an increasingly important trend as it is a scarce factor in locational competition. We thus expect the mobility of the high skilled to be largely supply determined.

Generally speaking, those who come for labour market reasons – the unskilled and highly skilled – usually have particularly favourable socio-demographic characteristics. We can expect them to be on average younger, more independent, less risk averse and more forward looking than the average.

Why do we need a (common) migration policy?

International migration of labour – together with international trade and the liberalisation of capital flows – is an essential instrument of economic integration which aims to enhance international competitiveness and to improve the international allocation of factor flows. Mobility of labour is important and necessary to exploit the benefits of economic integration that emanate from comparative advantage, increased specialisation and a more complete division of labour. This is why it is one of the four essential "freedoms" of a Common Market along with free trade of goods , free trade services and free mobility of capital.

Why migration is good
There are basically five reasons for the wealth enhancing importance of migration in economic integration:

1 Labour migration may make up for the fact that trade is not "perfect"
Mundell (1957) demonstrated that in a neo-classical world of the Heckscher-Ohlin-Samuelson (H-O-S) type[16] labour migration may substitute for hampered trade. In other words, if trade is not allowed to fully exploit the potential benefits of economic integration fully, for instance because it is impossible or too costly due to transport and transaction costs like tariff or non-tariff barriers to trade, then labour migration "can do the job" instead.

2 Trade and services tend to be complements
This is because trade of services is often only possible if the service provider moves too.

3 Where there is imperfect competition, movement of labour may be needed.
If the basis of exploiting gains from international integration is not to be found in H-O-S type differences in factor endowments but in imperfect competition or differences in production technology, both, trade and movement of labour (and capital flows) will have to complement each others in order to allow for full economic integration (Markusen, 1983).[17]

4 Local economies of scale may require it
If local economies of scale allow for more efficient production, the degree of labour mobility (and people's willingness to move where scale economies may be realised) can become an important determinant of development (Krugman, 1991a,b).

5 It can help cope with economic "shocks"
If highly developed and specialised economies experience macroeconomic shocks, labour mobility can be an effective and efficient short-run adjustment mechanism avoiding persistent unemployment increases and structural problems (Blanchard and Katz, 1992; European Economy, 1990).[18]

In brief, migration is overall wealth-enhancing, – if people move due to economic incentives.[19] Once trade, capital flows and migration have allowed for perfect economic integration and hence optimal allocation of factor flows, economic incentives will disappear and (net) migration will automatically come to a halt. Whether and how much mobility of labour is needed to achieve such an optimal situation will depend on the relative costs of trade, capital mobility and labour migration.

From an (allocational) economic point of view, there is thus good reason to welcome economically motivated migrants. Clearly, the best migration policy would be a laissez-faire policy of free movement of labour that did not distort economic incentives for migration. Who would like to come, has the means to come and is able legally to make his or her living should be allowed to do so as long as he or she wants. Irrespective of where they come from, the immigrants activity will increase overall economic wealth. However, this is only true, if markets are not seriously distorted and if there are no incentives to come or to stay that are of a non-allocative nature (for example, tax avoidance or incentives to stay for social benefit regulations).

The case against a laissez-faire approach
Apart from the purely allocational aspects summarised above, migration also has distributional consequences. Migration creates "winners" and "losers".

In the short run, the main "winners" of immigration will be owners of capital and native labour whose skills are complementary to those of the immigrants (or who work in jobs that are complementary to immigrant occupations). The main losers tend to be people who are similar to the immigrants and whose jobs may be substituted by immigrant occupations. While "winners" will find their opportunities and returns increase due to immigration even in the short run, the employment and gross wages of "losers" will decrease.[20] This implies transitory changes in the structure of society.[21]

If the overall economic benefits of immigration are positive, it would be theoretically possible to let "winners" "winners" compensate the "losers" But distributional effects may also have social consequences that are difficult to correct. In practice, compensation of "losers" often turns out to be difficult for political-economic reasons, especially if migration takes place rapidly. This is one reason why an optimal migration policy is unlikely to be totally laissez-faire. It is likely to be desirable to restrict immigration and reduce migration potential in the countries of origin when there are huge economic differences between the sending and the receiving economies.[22] The design of a migration policy should preferably include automatic mechanisms to compensate potential "losers".

Generally speaking, we would expect that the higher the substitutability of foreign for domestic workers, the more important will be the design of a (restrictive) immigration policy that defines entry and exit rules and supports the optimal allocation of immigrant labour once admitted. Such a policy must take account of the fact that there will always be categories of immigrants for whom the advantage of "taking them in" is by far larger than their costs of admission. This is most likely for high skilled workers and highly qualified professionals who are now and will continue to be scarce in the EU. It might be much cheaper to "roll out the red carpet for the skilled" than to build up these human resources within the EU.[23]

Another reason why restricting immigration may be desirable from the point of view of the welfare of the immigrant country is that being a citizen of a state is like membership in a club. Like clubs, states decide by themselves who belongs to them and who is a foreigner. Therefore, being a member of a state or a club is something very valuable. Indeed, the phenomenon of international migration is characterised by a legal asymmetry. In general, a country of origin is denied the right to close its borders to bona fide emigrants by the Universal Declaration of Human Rights.[24] However, a country of immigration has the undisputed right to decide whom and how many people it admits.[25]

In a club, one shares common goods (and values). Allowing new members to enter is important for the financing of these goods and the survival of the club, but if membership grows too rapidly, the system is likely to come under pressure, congestion effects may occur and eventually threaten the survival of the club in its original form.

We can summarise the policy-consequences of our discussion of benefits and costs of immigration by stating that:

a Due to distributional consequences of immigration and the value of citizenship as a 'club good' a laissez-faire policy of totally free migration is unlikely to be socio-economically optimal.

b A migration policy is needed in order to define clear entry and exit rules on the basis that a location should be open for immigration to the extent that immigrants' marginal productivity (labour market productivity, capital investments and their contribution to the financing of the societal public and club goods) is higher then their marginal costs of adaptation and natives' disutility from allowing them to join the club.

c The need for an efficient immigration policy that restricts entrance but allows those who are needed to come in and to stay, grows in times when social costs are rising and economic benefits are declining.

d To design an efficient migration policy we have to take the growing competition for scarce human resources into account. Migration policies have to be attractive for those who bring benefits for the economy and society. Even though immigration of the unskilled may be largely demand based, immigration of the high skilled is more likely to be supply determined. Neither closing the border completely, nor opening it for everybody is the goal, but a selection of those whose entrance is permitted, according to their benefits and costs for the immigration country.

e   An important element of the "internal" part of migration policy is to make sure that economic incentives for foreign labour allocation are not distorted by market failures and wrong incentives like tax avoidance or social benefit considerations.

f   An efficient "internal" migration policy has also to include measures to improve labour market flexibility. The best migration policy is a good labour market policy.

Why a common European EU policy?

But why, for all that, do we need a common European migration policy? There are two clear answers on this question. The first is economic, "internal" migration policy oriented and the second is more political, external "foreign" migration policy-oriented.

From the internal point of view, we have demonstrated that free mobility of labour is an important precondition for the exploitation of the benefits of economic integration. This is not only true for the inhabitants of a common market but also for third country immigrants. Henceforth, third country immigrants should not only be granted free mobility within a member country, but within the whole common market. If we allow for different migration policies within the same common market and do not grant free mobility to third country nationals, different policies work like different taxes. Separate immigration policies and immobility of third country nationals between member countries of a common market give room for strategic action, distort comparative advantage and hamper efficient factor allocation. Nationally independent migration policy and inter-country immobility of third country nationals are in permanent conflict with the goals of the Single European Market.[26] As a solution, one could grant third country nationals free mobility and leave nation states the sovereign right to define entry regimes. But provided that market mechanisms work this would mean that the country with the most open entry regulation would, implicitly, set the policy for the common market as a whole.

The "external" argument for a common migration policy is that we do not only deal with economically motivated immigrants. More and more, people flee from political persecution and ecological catastrophes. Resulting requests for admission are difficult to neglect purely on grounds of lack of economic demand. Welcoming people on humanitarian and ethical grounds is often costly, more costly and inefficient than to take action to prevent the "root-causes" of forced migration. Also, there is unfortunately little prospect of fast development convergence between the developed and less developed world. The number of those disadvantaged people in the South and East who dream of moving for a better living but lack the opportunity to do so (because they are not economically "wanted" in the North) is bound to increase. This creates at least moral arguments for helping to reduce migration potential in the South and East. For policy action and political pressure to oppose and prevent such migration pressure, however, unilateral action of single countries is inferior to joint action of the EU from the point of effectiveness and bargaining power. This is the simple argument about the need for a external "foreign" component of a common European migration policy.

Building a common EU migration policy

What has been done?
The elementary relationship between economic integration, migration and welfare was one of the basic ideas behind the common market which the European Community started to strive for in the mid-fifties. The original Treaty of Rome of 25 March 1957 which established the European Economic Community contains provision for the free movement of labour in Articles 48 *et seq*. Article 48 stipulates that "freedom of movement for workers" entails the "abolition of any discrimination based on nationality between workers of the member states as regards employment, remuneration and other conditions of work and employment". This right of free movement has been successively extended to the self-employed and to grant EU-wide freedom for the supply of services, including things like insurance. Furthermore, the treaty of Maastricht as it has been agreed upon on 2 February 1992, introduces the Union Citizenship, according to which every citizen of an EU member state is automatically also a citizen of the European Union. This citizenship incorporates different duties and rights. To the latter belong the right of freedom of movement and residence within the whole union and the active and passive right to participate in municipality elections in whatever member country an EU citizen takes residence. The Union citizenship can be seen as a logical development of the originally purely economically motivated free labour mobility into a basic political right of freedom of movement. It represent an essential step towards a "Europe of citizens".[27] Its further development will be one of the key issues in the so called "Maastricht II" Inter-Governmental Conference that is being negotiated in 1996-97.

What has been completely neglected in building up the EEA and the EU are the migration flows from and to the outside world. Third country citizens are not free to move within the EEA. Entering another EU country, they are still treated as if they had entered from outside of the EU. Furthermore, EU member states remain completely free to define their policy against migrants from the outside. They may independently set entry and exit rules and agree on bilateral agreements. Also, they are more or less free to decide on rights and duties of third country nationals. At present the EU has no active common migration policy. In many EU countries the national migration policy is basically limited to the setting of entry rules for third country nationals. So far, the only binding provision of co-operation in the field of migration policy towards third country nationals is the obligation of mutual information on new policy measures introduced.

The treaty of Maastricht contains some provisions that may give ground for designing a common European migration policy. Article K1 of the Treaty names immigration policy and the policy towards third countries as an issue of common interest. Migration policy has been attached to the task of co-operation in internal affairs and matters of administration of justice.

Furthermore, the Maastricht treaty says that the EU could be given binding competence to develop and implement a common EU-migration policy, but it requires unanimous decision-making for it. The intergovernmental conference will determine whether the basis for such a common migration policy will be developed. As long as it is not, the third country immigrants policy issue will remain in permanent conflict with the goals of the Single European Market.[28]

What should be done
So far we have tried to demonstrate that migration policy is not a threat to be feared. There is little ground to fear mass-immigration from third countries because the potential consists mainly of people who will find it hard to migrate, due to a lack in demand for their labour. In the European countries, immigration of unskilled and medium skilled is to a large extend demand based. But there is growing scope for competition in terms of immigration of scarce high skilled specialists. In brief, migration policy is a field that is still vastly uncovered by actual policy making. Once taken up for innovative, efficient design, it could contribute decisively to a further realisation of the welfare gains from economic integration and the success of European Integration. Issues of migration and "migration pressure" are likely to remain important in the future which makes it wise to deal with them in time.

```
┌─────────────────────────────────────────────────────────┐
│                    Common                                │
│               Migration Policy                           │
│                                                          │
│   Internal                    External 'foreign'         │
│   Migration Policy            Migration policy           │
│                                                          │
│   • rules of entry            • policy measures against  │
│   • rules of exit and           third countries in order │
│     eventual re-entrance        to oppose the creation of│
│   • rights and duties of        politically motivated    │
│     immigrants within the       migrants and refugees    │
│     whole of the common       • policy measures in the   │
│     market                      field of foreign policy  │
│   • 'keeping economic           and trade aiming to      │
│     incentives right'           reduce migration         │
│   • promotion of internal       potential in source      │
│     mobility and working of     countries                │
│     local labour markets      • co-ordinated and         │
│   • information about and       conditioned aid and      │
│     monitoring of migration     measures of              │
│     and labour market issues    development co-          │
│                                 operation to reduce      │
│                                 migration potential in   │
│                                 source countries         │
└─────────────────────────────────────────────────────────┘
```

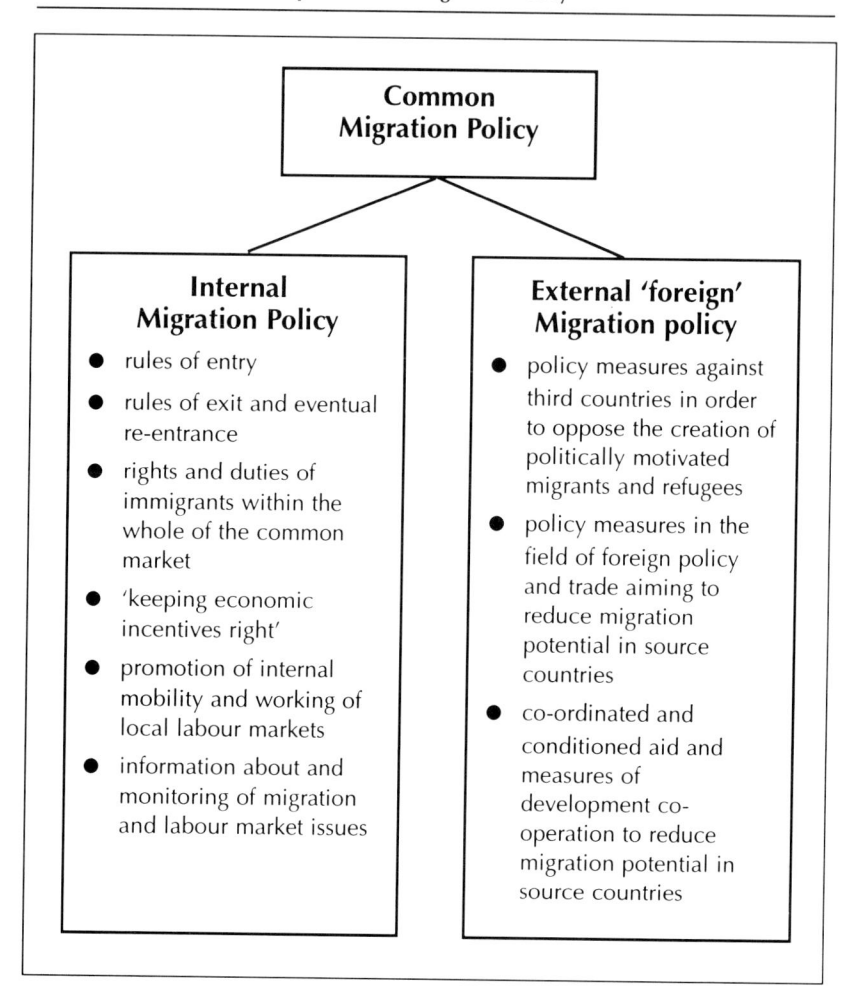

Fig. 3.10: Elements of an efficient migration policy

In our opinion, a migration policy should consist of two separate (but interdependent) parts: (a) an internal migration policy and (b) an external "foreign" migration policy (Fig. 3.10).

The internal migration policy has to define rules:

- restricting entry in a way that increases societal welfare and incorporates a minimum of distortion of economic incentives to migrate

- on exit and eventual re-entrance

- specifying rights and duties of third-country nationals within the whole of the common market

- to stimulate internal mobility and the working of local labour markets

- to provide and co-ordinate information about migration and labour market issues

The task of the external "foreign" migration policy would be to:

- take and co-ordinate policy measures designed to prevent the creation of politically motivated emigration and escape from third countries

- agree on policy measures in the field of foreign policy and trade aiming to reduce migration potential in the potential source countries

- co-ordinate and condition measures of development co-operation designed to reduce migration potential in the source countries

According to the principle of subsidiarity, not all of the envisaged measures necessarily have to be carried out at the common EU level.

Different targets may be followed in designing policies with regard to the above issues. In what follows, we do not discuss the issue of accepting immigrants on humanitarian grounds whose acceptance is determined by non-economic considerations.[29] Once they are allowed in, however, basically the same rules should apply to them as for economically motivated immigrants.

Ten guidelines for a new policy

From an economic point of view, we would like to suggest the following ten guidelines for the design of a common EU-migration policy:

1. **Let the markets decide who should be allowed in.** Economically motivated migration increases overall wealth in the country of immigration. Those immigrants who are most beneficial to the receiving country are those who are most scarce and therefore most needed. If overall immigration has to be restricted, partial agreements of free labour movement are likely to be the most economically

efficient because they do not select immigrants on criteria other than geographical and cultural proximity.

2. If targets for the numbers of immigrants allowed in mean that we do not want to grant freedom of immigration, it is best to **levy a fee or tax on entry** to restrict immigration rather than to allow immigrants in on arbitrary selection criteria. The fee may be used to compensate potential "losers", to finance migration policy measures or may be paid back if the migrant leaves the country again.

3. The general advise to reduce immigration is to **increase entry costs and to reduce the costs of return migration.**

4. **Once allowed in, apply the same rights and duties to immigrants** as to natives. In order to insure economic efficiency of immigrant labour allocation, do not restrict immigrants' rights to change jobs or move within the common market from one location and one employer to another. Third country nationals have to be entitled to move freely within the whole common market.

5. **Get the economic incentives for migration right.** Reduce barriers and obstacles to mobility. Eliminate non-allocative incentives for migration like tax and social security avoidance. Ease return migration and facilitate re-entry to those who consider returning home. Allow people in who can prove they are needed but do not at first give them special support if they find it difficult to make their living. An idea could be that during a starting period (say the first two years) immigrants should be excluded from unemployment benefit or similar kinds of social welfare payments. If they afterwards consider re-migrating, allow them to transfer their eventual rights to unemployment benefits or sickness leave to their next place of residence.

6. **Encourage integration of immigrants** who managed to successfully stay in the host country by easing access to political rights and eventual naturalisation.

7. **Be attractive for immigration of high skilled key-personnel.** Immigration of high skilled is likely to be of key importance for international competitiveness and the building up of Europe's human resources of tomorrow. But do not let migration policy of the EU become too discriminating. Racism and xenophobia are definitely self-

defeating, because they repulse the kind of (complementary) human resources Europe certainly will need.

8. **The best internal migration policy is a good labour market policy.** Improve the flexibility and working of local labour markets. Make appropriate information easily accessible. Correct other policy measures (eg public or housing loan systems and support programmes) that make people immobile.

9. **Increase prospects for economic development in countries with high migration potentials.** The best policy to reduce migration potential is to promote general growth prospects in (potential) migrant sending countries and not just to implement measures directed to discourage emigration.[30] Even if expectations about future development at home improve, migration potential will decrease. Growth promoting "foreign" migration policy measures can include improved market access for export goods, assistance to improve the working and international integration of financial markets, encouragement of technology diffusion and, last but not least, the promotion of "good governance" in migrant sending countries.[31] Be aware, however, that in very poor countries development may initially lead to an increase in migration propensities. Also, in some cases, improved information through investment activities may result in increased emigration to the investor country.[32]

10. Support efforts in stabilising the political systems in the emigration countries. Use co-ordinated multilateral (EU-)bargaining power to keep governments in potential sending countries from creating politically motivated emigration and escape. Promote the development of democratic tools and the installation of minority rights to prevent and handle internal conflicts. Another important contribution could be strict control and abolition of trade in arms and weapons in unstable world regions.

Conclusions

In this paper we have undertaken a synthesis of the implications of migration theory and presented some empirical evidence to argue against the formulation of purely defensive national migration policies driven by fears of mass-immigration. Although the migration potential in some less developed countries are likely to grow, immigration of unskilled or semi-skilled migrants from third countries is largely demand based. Those who would like to come are often not those who can come because the lack of demand for their labour makes it impossible for them to move and to make their living in European immigration countries. A more innovative, forward looking migration policy is needed, however, because labour mobility can make important contributions to the further proceeding of economic integration in the EU and to future economic development.

Migration and labour mobility are economically efficient and increase overall wealth, provided the economic incentives are set right. Distributional aspects of immigration, however, make it unlikely that a completely free laissez-faire immigration policy towards the rest of the world will be socially optimal. Nevertheless, some immigration of unskilled persons will continue to be economically needed. Immigration of the high skilled is likely to become an important issue in the determination of locational competitiveness and regional attractivity. Within the EU, low labour mobility rather than mass immigration represents a problem for future integration.

If migration has to be restricted in some way, the explicit formulation of a migration policy is needed, an internal migration policy setting rules on entry, exit and rights and duties for all migrants within the common market and an external 'foreign' migration policy co-ordinating and implementing measures to reduce migration potential in sending countries. A common EU migration policy is needed because granting third country immigrants free movement within the whole of the common market is an essential requirement to realise the goals of full economic integration incorporated in the Single Market programme and because allowing free movement of third-country nationals within the EEA without a common migration policy means that the member country with the most open policy implicitly sets the rules for the entire market. An external common EU "foreign" migration policy is needed because, unilateral action of single countries is inferior to joint multilateral action from point of view of effectiveness and bargaining power.

This analysis leads to a number of policy proposals. It is these guidelines that need to be followed for the formulation of an efficient and forward-looking common European migration policy.

Endnotes

1. The impact of the changing demographic trend in Central European societies and the (restricted) possibility for immigration to compensate for that trend are discussed eg in Steineck (1994), Zimmermann (1991), Masson and Tryon (1990), Hagemann and Nicoletti (1989), Bös and Weizsäcker (1989) and OECD (1988). Coleman (1991:18) asking whether there is a need for immigration concludes that "increased immigration is not needed to satisfy quantitative workforce deficiencies at least for the next ten or twenty years in Western Europe or the EC in general." His result is based on the substantial reserves of employable manpower which greatly exceed any short-term demographic deficiencies. "The current number of unemployed alone is equivalent to the demographic deficit beyond the first decade of the next century" (Coleman 1991:18). As the literature on the impact of demographic transition on migration demand has already been lively debated, we will concentrate on the other arguments in what follows.
2. These categories have been originally developed by Maslow (1972) and Allardt (1975).
3. See eg Fischer, Martin and Straubhaar (1995) for a recent evaluation.
4. Faist (1995) presents a remarkable attempt to survey and synthesise sociological and political micro and macro theories of migration.
5. The conclusion that the demand for migration of high skilled will increase implicitly assumes that the enhancing effects of economic integration and local specialisation are not outweighed by decreases in transportation and transaction costs and advancements in communication reducing the requirement for specialists to move to a certain place. From a more micro point of view, the analysis of multinational companies derives similar conclusions. Salt notes: "What this means is that as the organization becomes multinational, it increasingly uses relocated skills and expertise to exercise control from the centre; but after a certain point the trend toward the international relocation of staff is halted and may well go into reverse" (Salt, 1992:501).
6. Our neglect of 'new forms of mobility' (Majava, 1991) that are less tied to economic (labour market) needs, like the temporary movement of people for reasons of education or pensioners moving for natural amenities, does not imply that we consider such forms of mobility less important for migration in EU countries. Our discussion has just concentrated on economically determined and work related reasons for migration. We believe this kind of migration to be most important for the determination of (restricted) immigration from third countries into the EU.
7. Where not otherwise stated, all the following data is taken from Eurostat (1996).
8. For Luxembourg, the data refers to 1991.
9. If not otherwise stated, all the following UK figures are calculated from HMSO (1995) and CSO (1990, 1995). Note that for Britain there are sometimes non-trivial differences in data on migration and migrants, depending on the respective source. See for example the appendix in Salt (1995) for a more detailed technical description of sources.

10 Furthermore, intra-company migration was of outmost importance. According to Salt (1995), no less than 43.5 per cent of all foreign national labour immigrating into the UK in 1994–95 changed workplace within the same (multinational) company. See also the chapter by Salt in this book.

11 The migration figures for Germany given here exclude Germans and thus also the so called 'Aussiedler', German origin "returnees" from the East, whose number amounted to approximately 2.3 million people between 1968 and 1994 (German Statistical Yearbooks). For further discussion of the peculiarities of immigration into Germany see the chapter by Hönekopp in this book.

12 To make the information comparable, we plotted all data in Fig. 3.8 as indices calculated with a base value of 1 for 1975. The graphs thus show variations relative to 1975.

13 Although one may argue that any really important relation between two variables should show up in a graphical presentation, one has of course to be cautious in drawing such kind of conclusions only on grounds of multi-variable graphics. For Italy, we have run a GLS-regression of (logarithms) of immigration rates against GDP and labour market indicators. The following variables were estimated to contribute to the determination of immigration rates at a probability level >0.95 per cent, listed with decreasing significance (in brackets the direction of the relation): unemployment rates in Germany(-), GDP per worker in Italy(-) and unemployment rates in Italy(+). Employment patterns in Germany and Italy did not contribute to explaining migration patterns. The results, however, suggested several problems with the data and estimation method.

14 Various more sound econometric analyses confirm the predominantly demand determined character of immigration from relatively lower developed Mediterranean countries into the EU. See Straubhaar (1988) for an in-depth analysis.

15 An H-O-S world is, above all, characterised by perfectly competitive markets and comparative advantage that results from locationally different factor endowments (only).

16 Admittedly, in some cases where the world is different from the H-O-S utopia, trade and free movement of factor flows may be inferior to unilateral strategic action in maximising national wealth. See Krugman (1987) for a discussion of the relevant literature. Krugman concludes, however, that "Free trade is not passé, but it is an idea that has irretrievably lost its innocence. Its status has shifted from optimum to reasonable rule of thumb" (Krugman, 1987; 132).

17 In a recent paper, Fatás & Decressin (1995) show that the EEA is indeed characterised by a particularly low labour mobility compared, for example, to the United States. Therefore, regional asymmetric shocks tend to have long run consequences and increase local unemployment persistently.

18 During recent years, a vast literature on the economic effects of labour mobility has emerged that goes far beyond what we present here. For a general introduction see Fischer and Straubhaar (1996) and the references therein.

19 Razin & Sadka (1995) argue that introducing migration in the presence of structural unemployment might indeed be wealth decreasing because it mainly results in a further increase of unemployment. To obtain this result, however, they have to make some rather questionable assumptions, for example that natives and immigrants are *de facto* perfect substitutes. Schmidt, Stilz and Zimmermann (1994) demonstrate that the consequences of immigration in the presence of structural unemployment crucially depend on the causes of the unemployment problem. Immigration may well help to overcome rigidities that cause unemployment and thereby improve the situation even of natives who tend to be in a substitutive relationship to immigrants.
20 For a more comprehensive discussion of distributional effects of migration Straubhaar (1992).
21 Furthermore, in the presence of scale economies, "factor mobility which is important in a regional economy like the common market could increase inter-regional inequality, if factors move to the high-return regions, characterized by a larger purchasing power and the benefits of higher productivity stemming from more favourable management and social structure. ... A too-rigid 'division of labour' between the North and the South, according to which the South specializes more in traditional labour-intensive industries, could be counter-productive" (Jacquemin, 1990;47-49).
22 This is exactly the question Markusen (1988) asked. For Canada his result is that the best thing an economy could do is to subsidise the use, not training, of skilled specialists. The latter policy would subsidise foreign economy through emigration of the skilled natives.
23 Of course, the right to "leave any country, including one's own" is not granted all over the globe. Many countries enforce more or less strict (re-)emigration regulations. Weiner (1985:444-445).
24 "Affluent and free countries are, like élite universities, besieged by applicants. They have to decide on their own size and character. More precisely, as citizens of such a country, we have to decide: Whom should we admit? Ought we to have open admissions?" Walzer (1983:32).
25 An excellent outline of the problem and first step towards a solution is given by Böhning and Werquin (1990).
26 However, the right of free movement is still not all encompassing. For example, it does not apply to the unemployed or to people who are dependent on other sorts of social welfare payments. This is to avoid a so called "social welfare tourism".
27 Another way to proceed towards a common migration policy might be on the basis of voluntary intergovernmental agreements between some EU countries which others may join later. The Schengen treaty on the abolition of border controls is such an example which could be transferred into binding EU law. Originally signed by Belgium, Germany, France, Luxembourg and the Netherlands in 1985 (I) and 1990 (II), Italy, Spain, Portugal Greece and Austria have joined in since. Denmark, Finland and Sweden are expected to officially sign in during summer 1996. The Schengen treaty is, however, above all about border controls, about co-operation by the different national police in matters of personal and tax control and about co-operation and exchange of information regarding asylum

and refugee policies, It does not really refer to migration policy making. The immigration pressure from the "would like to be Europeans" perhaps more than anything else, will test the EU intra-area willingness to co-operate and the hardiness of the intention to abolish frontiers. It is in the view of labour movements from the outside into the EU that the EU might become a "Fortress Europe".

28 Admittedly, the distinction between economic and political motivated migrants is often somewhat arbitrary. For many potential immigrants admittance on humanitarian grounds and admittance for economic reasons may represent two partially substitutive "entrance" doors to consider.

29 Note that once donor countries start to declare aid conditional on action taken to "reduce" migration potential, migration potential itself as well as its perception by potential immigrant countries becomes an issue of strategic interest for governments in potential sending countries which aim to enhance aid and development support received.

30 While simple aid transfers often establish dependency relationships and prevent markets from working rather than promoting sustainable development, the design and development of efficient economic policy and labour market institutions is conditional for growth enhancing market mechanisms to work. In this sense, supporting "good governance" often represents a key element in promoting growth prospects and thus reducing migration potential in source countries.

31 For a more detailed discussion and an optimistic assessment of the need for and feasibility of "aid in place of migration" see the chapter by Molle in this book.

References

Allardt E (1975) *About Dimensions of Welfare. An Exploratory Analysis of a Comparative Scandinavian Survey*. University of Helsinki, Research Group for Comparative Sociology.

Becker GS (1962) Investment in Human Capital. A Theoretical Analysis, *Journal of Political Economy* 70, Supplement.

Becker GS (1964) *Human Capital: A Theoretical and Empirical Analysis with special Reference to Education*, New York & London.

Berninghaus S & Seifert-Vogt HG (1992) "A microeconomic model of migration", in Zimmermann KF (Ed.) *Migration and Economic Development*, Springer, Berlin.

Blanchard OJ & Katz LF (1992) Regional Evolutions, *Brooking Papers on Economic Activity* 92/1.

Böhning WR (1995) "Top End and Bottom End Labour Import in the United States and Europe: Historical Evolution and Sustainability", in Böhning; de Beijl (Ed.)

Böhning WR & Werquin J (1990) Some Economic, Social and Human Rights Considerations Concerning the Future Sttus of Third-Country Nationals in the Single European Market. *World Employment Programme Working Paper* 46. International Labour Office, Geneva.

Bös D & Weizsäcker R (1989) Economic Consequences of an Ageing Population, *European Economic Review* 33.

Chiswick BR (1986) Is the new Immigration less skilled than the old?, *Journal of Labour Economics* 4.

Coleman D (1991) *Demographic Projections: is there a Need for Immigration?* Paper prepared for the Conference on "The New Europe and International Migration", Giovanni Agnelli Foundation, Turin, Novembre 25-27, 1991, *mimeo*.

Coleman D (1995) "The United Kingdom and International Migration: A Changing Balance", in Fassmann H & Manz R (Eds.) *European Migration in the Late Twentieth Century*, Edward Elgar, Aldershot.

CSO (1990) *Annual Abstract of Statistics* 126 HMSO, London.

CSO (1995) *Annual Abstract of Statistics* 131 HMSO, London.

European Economy (1990) *One Market, One Money* 44.

EUROSTAT (1996) *Migration Statistics*, Luxembourg.

Faini R. & Venturini A (1994) *Migration and Growth: the Experience of Southern Europe*, CEPR dp 906 London.

Faist Th (1995) "Sociological Theories of International Migration: the Missing Meso Link." ZeS dp, Bremen, forthcoming in: Hammer et al. (Ed.) *Migration, Immobility and Development*.

Fatás A & Decressin J (1995) "Regional Labor Market Dynamics in Europe", *European Economic Review* 39.

Findlay AM (1993) "New Technology, High-Level Labour Movements and the Concept of the Brain Drain", *The Changing Course of International Migration*, OECD, Paris.

Fischer PA., Martin R & Straubhaar Th (1995a) *Should I stay or should I go? Microeconomic Contributions towards a Multi-Disciplinary Theory of Migration* dp in Economic Policy no. 49, University of the Bundeswehr, Hamburg.

Fischer PA, Martin R & Straubhaar Th (1995b) *Development and Migration or Migration and Development. Macroeconomic Contributions towards a Multi-Disciplinary Theory of Migration.* dp in Economic Policy no. 57, University of the Bundeswehr, Hamburg.

Fischer PA & Straubhaar Th (1995) "Economic and Social Aspects of Immigration into Switzerland", in Fassmann H & Manz R (Eds.) *European Migration in the Late Twentieth Century*, Edward Elgar, Aldershot.

Fischer PA & Straubhaar Th (1996) *Migration and Economic Integration in the Nordic Common Labour Market*, Nordic Council of Ministers, Copenhagen.

Ghatak S & Levine P (1993) *Migration Theory and Evidence: An Assessment*, CEPR Discussion Paper 769, London.

Hagemann R & Nicoletti G (1989) *Ageing Populations: Economic Effects and Implications for Public Finance*, Department of Economics and Statistics Working Paper 61, Paris: OECD.

Hammar T et al (1994) *Migration, Population and Poverty: A Theoretical and Empirical Project on South-North Migration and the Immigration Control Policies of Industrialised Countries*, Center of Research in International Migration and Ethnic Relations, University of Stockholm.

Harris JR & Todar MP (1970) "Migration, Unemployment and Development: A Two-Sector Analysis" *American Economic Review* 60.

Herzog, Schlottmann and Boehm (1993) "Migration as Spatial Job-Search: A Survey of Empirical Findings", *Regional Studies*, vol.27, pp.327–340.

HMSO (1995) *International migration – migrants entering or leaving the United Kingdom and England and Wales* Office of Population Censuses and Surveys, HMSO, London.

ILO/IOM/UNHCR (1994) *Migrants, Refugees and International Cooperation*

IOM (International Organization for Migration) (1991) Ninth IOM Seminar on Migration: South-North Migration. *International Migration* 29.

Jacquemin A (1990) "Comment on Neven", *Economic Policy* 5.

Krugman P (1987) "Is Free Trade Passé?", *Journal of Economic Perspectives* 1.

Krugman P (1991a) *Geography and Trade*, Leuven.

Krugman P (1991b) "Increasing Returns and Economic Geography", *Journal of Political Economy*, vol.99 no. 3.

Krugman P (1995) Growing World Trade: Causes and Consequences, *Brooking Papers on Economic Activity*, 1, pp.327–377

Lee ES (1966) "A Theory of Migration" *Demography* 3(1).

Majava A (1991) "Towards an Equitable Sharing of the Benefits of International Migration", *Yearbook of Population Research in Finland*, 29:93-8, Helsinki.

Markusen JR (1988) "Production, Trade and Miugration with Differentiated, Skilled Workers", *Canadian Journal of Economics* 21.

Maslow AH (1972) *Motivation and Personality* Harper and Row, New York.

Massey DS et al (1993) "Theories of Internation Migration: A Review and Appraisal", *Population and Development Review* 19.

Masson PR & Tryon RW (1990) *Macroeconomic Effects of Projected Population Aging in Industrial Countries*, IMF Staff Papers 37.

McCall BP & McCall JJ (1987) "A sequential study of migration and job search", *Journal of Labor Economics*, 5, pp.452–476

Mundell RA (1957) "International Trade and Factor Mobility", *American Economic Review* 47.

OECD (1988) *Ageing Populations: The Social Policy Implications*, Paris.

Razin A & Sadka E (1995) *Resisting Migration: Wage Regidity and Income Distribution*, CEPR dp 1091, London.

Salt J (1992) "Migration Processes among the Highly Skilled in Europe" *International Migration Review* 26.

Salt J (1995a) *International Migration and the United Kingdom* Report of the UK correspondent to the SOPEMI, OECD, Paris.

Salt J (1995b) "Foreign Workers in the United Kingdom", *Employment Gazette* January, London.

Salt J & Singleton A (1995) "The International Migration of Expertise: The Case of the United Kingdom", *Studi Emigrazione/Etudes Migrations* 32.

Schmidt Ch M, Stilz A & Zimmmermann KF (1994) "Mass Migration, Unions and Government Intervention" *Journal of Public Economics* 55.

Sjaastad L (1962) "The Cost and Returns of Human Migration" *Journal of Political Economy* 70.

Stark O (1991) *The Migration of Labor*, Cambridge: Basil Blackwell.

Stark O & Bloom DE (1985) "The New Economics of Labour Migration", *American Economic Review*, Papers & Proceedings, 75.

Stark O & Taylor JE (1989) "Relative deprivation and international migration", *Demography* 26.

Steineck A (1994) *Ökonomische Anfordreungen an eine europäische Zuwanderungspolitik* Nomos (Ed.), Baden-Baden (Germany).

Straubhaar Th (1988) *On the Economics of International Labor Migration*, Bern: Haupt.

Straubhaar Th (1992) "Allocational and Distributional Aspects of Future Immigration into Western Europe", *International Migration Review* 26.

Straubhaar Th (1993) "Migration Pressure", *International Migration* 31/1.

Summers & Heaston (1994) *World Penn Tables*, University of Pennsylvania.

Walzer M (1983) *Spheres of Justice*, New York, Basic Books.

Weiner M (1985) "On International Migration and International Relations", *Population and Development Review* 11.

Westin Ch (1994) *Immigration to Sweden 1943-1993 and the Response of the Public Opinion*. Paper presented at the 84th annual Meeting of the Society for the Advancement of Scandinavian Studies, Davenport, Iowa

Zimmermann KF (1991) "Ageing and the Labor Market. Age Structure, Cohort Size and Unemployment", *Journal of Population Economics* 4.

4. The contribution of international aid to the long-term solution of the European migration problem
Willem Molle[1]

Introduction

The Migration Problem

Immigration is considered to be a problem by all the countries of north western Europe. This is not merely a political fact: economic analysis tells us that the long-run net welfare effects of international mass-migration are highly uncertain for both the sending and the receiving country. Reduction of mass-migration is consequently seen as a desirable policy goal.

Most of the policies that are now debated as potential solutions to this problem take a short-term view. They tend to focus on the setting of rules about entry conditions. While such policies may be very justified to cope with immediate problems, they let us forget about the long-term solution which is the taking away of the stimuli for migration.

Migration of labour in Europe is motivated by many factors, that can be classified as either push factors (for instance the political situation in the sending country) or pull factors (like higher wage levels in the receiving country). Among these, economic factors, in practice differences in both access to jobs and in wage levels between Western Europe on the one hand and the major sending areas on the other hand, take pride of place.

Wage differences between South and East and the West[2] are very large, so if migration were free, a considerable amount of immigration to the West would occur.

The reduction of the wealth gap will only come about as a consequence of a catching-up process of the South and East with the West. This means that economic growth in the sending countries has to be significantly higher than the growth rate of the receiving countries over a considerable period of time.

The resources of the countries of the South and East are insufficient to bring this about. International aid would accelerate the catching-up process. The question we intend to answer in this paper is what magnitude, form, content and dimensions foreign aid would have to have in order to reduce the pressure on the labour market of the major emigration countries to such an extent that large-scale migration from these countries to western Europe would not occur.

In principle we know that international aid is conducive to the reduction of the pressure for migration and can play an important role; two illustrations of such a connection between economic performance, aid and the decrease in migration can be given.

- In the first decade after the Second World War high unemployment prevailed in western Europe. Many people who saw insufficient opportunities in the countries of Western Europe emigrated to the United States, Canada and Australia. During the fifties the economic situation in western Europe changed dramatically, for a large part as a consequence of aid given through the Marshall plan. Emigration stopped as a consequence also.

- In the sixties and beginning of the seventies many people from southern European countries like Spain, Portugal, and Greece migrated to the north west of Europe filling in many job opportunities created by fast economic growth. However, after these countries became member of the EU their growth rates accelerated quickly as a consequence of the improved market access and the massive inflow of aid from the structural funds. Increased job opportunities and higher wealth levels made that out migration sharply fell and return migration even set in. This was enhanced by the fact that EU citizenship guaranteed the access to the labour market of partner countries at any moment, so returning did not mean the loss of opportunities.

The problem and its solutions
Migration into north western Europe comes mostly from three sources:

1 *The southern and eastern rim of the Mediterranean sea.* Traditionally immigration from this area was for work reasons. Nowadays this area sends a considerable number of emigrants to the West on the basis of family reunification.

2   *Central and eastern Europe.* The opening up of the formerly centrally planned economies to the world market has had a big influence on the possibilities of migration for people from these countries. In the last five years the numbers of migrants from the East have become very considerable.

3   *Developing Countries.* As a consequence of better communications the inflow of migrants from this source has considerably increased. The number of asylum seekers and illegal entrants has become very important as well.

The increased pressure from immigration into the West has created a growing unwillingness among the western population to accept further immigration (as the Eurobarometer surveys have shown).

Consequently, migration is a point of major concern to most governments in the European Union. Most of the discussion on migration policy is about the ways in which systems of control can be made effective in limiting the number of incoming migrants. In all countries of the EU restrictive migration policies are advocated and implemented. These policies are however far from homogeneous: each country has its own set of rules. The reason is that the EU has no regulatory power in the field of immigration and the Treaty of Maastricht has not brought significant changes on this score (Molle 1994).

In what follows, we leave to one side the debate on the best policy to restrict migration in the short run and focus on the long-run. That means that we need to analyse how policy can help the sending countries speed up their economic growth so as to alleviate the pressure of migration in the long run. Two major sets of policy can be distinguished as ways to enhance growth.

Improving market access
This means that the West lowers its import barriers to the products coming from the countries of the South and East. Complementary to this is a policy by which the West stimulates the flow of private capital to the countries of South and East since direct investment will enhance the development of modern industries and the transfer of technology. The final part of this set of policies is to support the integration of the economies of the sending countries in a regional co-operation network. The EU has shown that it is ready to work along these lines. In recent years it has formalised the policy with respect to the East in the Association Agreements, that imply a progressive liberalisation of trade between the EU and the East and

eventually the participation of the East in the internal market of the EU leading to a full membership of eastern countries of the EU (see CEC 1994). For the South the efforts have been in the form of co-operation agreements, permitting tariff-free entrance of many of their exports into the EU market. For the future, the objective is a fully fledged Free Trade Area, encompassing the whole of the EU and the Mediterranean area. Accession to the EU however is not on the cards for these countries.

Aid to enhance structural adaptation
These involve the transfer of financial, human and other resources from the West to the South and East. The EU has considerable experience in the pursuit of such policies. As a matter of fact, it has a long-standing policy towards the Less Developed Countries, a policy of more recent origin in terms of eastern Europe (PHARE/TACIS), and a very recently agreed policy for the South (MEDA).

The policy of opening up markets and their effects on migration have been extensively analysed and we will not go into them here. We concentrate our attention on aid policies aimed at promoting structural improvement of the production capacity of the South and East.

To analyse these issues we take four steps. First, we analyse the patterns of migration into Europe, its causes and its economic impact. Next, we analyse the way in which foreign aid is capable of improving the conditions in the major sending countries. Third, we describe the different policy options, evaluate the gap in economic performance that needs be closed and specify the factors that stimulate growth. Finally, we describe the present programmes of the EU of structural aid to the South and the East.

Since much attention has been paid to the macro-economic and international economic aspects of aid programmes, we concentrate on labour market and educational policy programmes. This is justified because the improvement of the quality of the labour supply is considered one of the most important factors stimulating economic growth. Finally, we will draw some general conclusions from our analysis.

Migration analysis

Migration trends
In the course of history there have been a number of periods of mass-migration. Of these movements, only the fairly recent ones have shaped the present migration problem in Europe.

The first occurred during the sixties, when north-western European countries began a large-scale recruitment of labour from southern Europe and the northern part of Africa (Molle and Van Mourik, 1988). In the 1970s this policy was stopped. However, in the following decades the consequences of it came to light in the form of new waves of migrants, both legal, as a consequence of family reunification, and illegal, based on networks.

The migration from the South is fairly well documented. The patterns of migration are dominated by Turks moving to Germany and north Africans moving to France and Belgium. Considerable numbers of guest-workers from northern Africa remained in Western Europe and family members joined them at a later stage. Migration from Turkey and Morocco to the Netherlands, for example, was during the 1980s, three to five times higher than the flow in the opposite direction. In recent years only one per cent of the Moroccan and two per cent of the Turkish population in the Netherlands returned to their home country every year. In contrast, those from Spain and Portugal returned home for the larger part at the beginning of the 1980s when the economic situation in their home country became more favourable following accession to the EU.

The political and economic events in the former Soviet bloc at the end of the 1980s have given rise to a new wave of migration, this time from eastern to western Europe. These flows consist for a large part of repatriating Germans (*Aussiedler*). Other migrants are asylum-seekers and tourists who extend their stay in western countries, with the purpose either of finding (temporary) employment and for seeking permanent residence. The most important sending countries are Poland and Yugoslavia, and in recent years the former Soviet Union. Germany is by far the most important country of destination for migrants, not only for the *Aussiedler*, but also for other migrants. The scarce information that is available on the characteristics of these migrants shows that the majority are young and middle aged well-educated people[3]. Many arrive on a temporary basis, but try to extend their stay in the West[4].

The question is how many of these migrants from the East to the West will go back after some time to their countries of origin. There are two reasons why a comparison with the southern European group might be more appropriate in helping us answer this question than with the north African group:

- the starting level of *per capita* income in the East is closer to that of the southern European countries than that of the north African countries

- the countries of the East have the prospect of becoming members of the EU, and thereby acquiring the freedom to move within the whole area; the north African countries do not have this perspective

Welfare effects

The economic analysis of migration is fairly complicated. In terms of economic welfare the effects are quite different for the recipient and for the sending countries.

Receivers

The impact of migration on the economy of the recipient countries can be measured by various indicators, like unemployment, industrial restructuring, wage levels, income distribution, contributions to and demands on public finance, flexibility of the labour market, sustainability of the social security system, and so on. The studies that have been made do not all agree. For the European case see Siebert 1994; Spencer 1994, Zimmermann 1995, and for the US: Borjas 1995 and Friedberg and Hunt 1995). Nevertheless, the conclusion seems to be that the gains from immigration to the receiving countries have on average been positive. However, the effects depend critically on the situation in the labour market. In the 1960s and 1970s, shortages in labour supply were a barrier to growth, hence migration had overall positive effects. At the moment all EU countries have to cope with high unemployment (notwithstanding labour shortages in some sectors and occupations) and with an ageing population, both indigenous and immigrant. Moreover, the problems of unemployment now tend to concentrate in the immigrant population[5] and hence grave problems like social exclusion and crime tend to accumulate (Molle and Zandvliet 1994). The policies that try to remedy this situation and enhance the chances for immigrants are costly and their effects are up till now limited (see Rettab 1996).

This means that the benefits from immigrants are likely to be much less than they were in the earlier period. This has led to the suggestion of limiting migration and following a strategic or selective immigration policy, whereby a liberal stance towards the young and better educated is operated and a restrictive policy is made towards other segments of population.

Senders

Migration has contradictory effects on the sending countries. The negative side is that it is mostly the young well-educated who leave, involving a loss for the country of essential segments of its human capital in which it has heavily invested and hence a loss of potential growth. The positive side to migration comes, firstly, from the use the home country makes of the remittances (cash transfer) paid back to it by migrant workers and, secondly, after the return of the migrant of the skills acquired abroad.

However, it is unclear whether these benefits are that large. Some studies indicate that the contribution of migrants to the economic performance of the home-country has probably been very moderate (Keely and Tran, 1989; see also for the Maghreb countries the contribution by Garson in OECD 1994).

Remittances have only been used to a limited extent to enlarge the productive capacity of the home-country. Indeed, most of it is spent on consumption, part on housebuilding, and an even smaller part on investment. Skills are not very well used either. Because most of the migrant workers are employed in low-skilled work the building up of skill is on average very poor. Moreover, (and apart from any psychological effects[6]) the picture foreign workers have got of the western market economy, working conditions, company organisation and risk taking is very special and biased. Working experience under these circumstances is unlikely to be beneficial to the home-country.

Push factors

Migration from countries in the South and the East comes both from economic and from non-economic factors. The most relevant factors are:

- *Economic*; there is little disagreement that the main push factors are primarily economic: low income, rising unemployment, lack of employment opportunities, the breakdown of old social security systems (in the East), little belief in future possibilities for employment and income, lack of (cheap) capital.

- *Demography*; in the coming period a substantial rise in the labour force is expected in many of the countries of the South and East.

- *Restructuring*; in the East considerable numbers have been laid off, and many of them have difficulty of finding stable employment in new activities. Moreover, in the East the restructuring process is far from finished. In the South, a number of countries have still to begin their structural adaptation process. The qualifications of the persons that are laid off seldom match those demanded by modern industries and service activities.

- *Government spending*; activities such as public administration, medical care, education, cultural activities, that depend on the state-budget might encounter a further loss of employment in the coming years, as a consequence of the growing problems governments have in balancing their budgets.

- *Spatial differences*; unemployment is comparatively high in small towns in rural areas and in regions with a monoculture in production.

- *Other factors*; Many things add to the motivation to migrate in both East and South: disbelief in government institutions, greater inequality in income distribution, lack of good housing, corruption, infringements of human rights, discrimination of ethnic and religious minorities, civil war (Yugoslavia), lack of education possibilities and a poor environment. The lack of belief in an improvement in this situation is an additional factor in the process of migration.

"Potential" migration leads to effective or actual migration when the push factors are strong enough to overcome the various barriers to migration. Often the difference in culture and language is mentioned in this respect. However, the west European recruitment of labour from countries with a totally different culture and language (the Arab countries) during the 1960s and 1970s shows that the argument that cultural differences and language are major barriers to migration may be overruled by the magnitude of the push factors. And indeed, many low or unskilled jobs do not require fluent speech.

Pull factors

The main pull factors are also economic and non-economic in nature.

- *Standard of living*; living standards in western Europe are much higher than those in wastern Europe and north Africa.

- *Demography*; the west European native population will stagnate and in some countries even decline in the next decades, as a consequence of low and mostly below replacement fertility rates. In all countries the average age will go up very significantly. It is an open question whether, with the resulting structure of the population, the social security system, old age pension schemes and health care systems can be financed in the near future. In the labour market, employers are confronted with a declining supply of young (cheap) labour.

- *Specific vacancies*; in the lower and unskilled segments of the labour market, there are not very many job opportunities, as a consequence of the excess supply of this category of labour in most western European countries. However, even for some low-skilled jobs employers have difficulty in finding workers, and they strongly plead for a less severe system of work permits for non-EU inhabitants.[7] When this is not granted, there is a strong incentive for employers to hire illegal workers. One has to keep in mind, however, that motives that drive the demand for illegal employees – the need for flexibility in labour supply and for lower costs – may also play a part in the (legal) demand for eastern European labour. Additionally, the lower costs of this labour might compensate for its possible lower productivity.

- *Migration chains*; immigrants established for some time in the country of destination (such as the tight-knit Polish communities in countries like Germany or the UK) are a source of information to potential immigrants and a bridgehead for new immigrants that settle in the country. Evidence from a study on the Dutch illegal labour-market (Zandvliet and Gravensteijn-Ligthelm 1994) suggests that a majority of illegal workers, mainly from the former recruitment countries of Turkey and Morocco, get a job through family or friends. Established immigrants permit the lowering of the cultural and language barriers and thereby reduce the hindrances to migration.

- *Underground economy*; many migrants accept wages and labour conditions well below normal western European standards. As a consequence of the limited demand for legal immigrant labour, many are willing to work at least temporarily, in the illegal labour market.[8] Among employers there are different motives for this demand:

Lower costs. This motive may be a result of:

    a   strong price competition in both local and international product markets. Most of the time, this concerns activities that would not survive in the western countries without cheap, migrant labour b   the need to increase profits. Poor working conditions permit employers to reduce costs below those of competitors

Problems in finding workers. Three categories can be distinguished:

a   skilled labour where supply falls short in the western countries

b   labour prepared to put up with comparatively bad working conditions, such as low payment below the minimum wage level, heavy physical labour (in agriculture and some industrial occupations), work in a poor environment (noise, bad air)

c   labour needed at irregular and/or unfavourable times, such as cleaning work at nights, or for short periods, such as seasonal labour in agriculture and tourism, but also peak production in other (industrial) activities

Conclusions

In conclusion we have seen that the migration phenomenon is based on a combination of push- and pull-factors, economic, demographic, social and political nature all of which interact. The influence of these different factors can not always be separated.

Given the conditions in both West, South and East there is a very large potential for South-West and for East-West migration. However, the magnitude of the actual flow of migrants in the coming one or two decades is hard to predict because of the unpredictability of the different determining factors.

Aid and development

Why Push factors are the key
Without policy intervention, it is likely that millions of people will migrate to western Europe in the coming decades. The net welfare effects of such large movements of population are not likely to be positive, either for the receiving or for the sending countries. It is not surprising therefore that policies to restrict migration are being designed; either aimed at the push and pull factors, or at the barriers to movement.

In terms of limiting the pull factors, the one policy preferred in the countries of western Europe is the attempt to limit the attraction to employers of filling vacancies with illegal immigrant labour. Two policy options could be envisaged. The first is to induce more of the local unemployed to accept the jobs involved, thereby decreasing the demand for migrant labour. However, experience shows that this policy is not very successful. The second is to deter employers from hiring (illegal) immigrants. However, as immigrants are generally willing to accept, by western standards, very low wages and bad working conditions, it is not very realistic to assume that the phenomenon can be stopped in this way.

Policies that approach the phenomenon via the barriers to migration, typically try to restrict the access to the country of destination by way of permits that can only be obtained through fulfilling certain criteria. Much of the debate on migration policy is actually on the issues related to the choice and application of these criteria. This type of policy is geared to solving the perceived short run problem. It does not give a real solution to the problem and can only artificially contain potential migration.

Diminishing the push factors in the sending countries by creating jobs and improving standards of living there, is the only real answer to the long-term problem. How should this be approached?

How large is the gap that needs to be bridged?

Differences
Differences in wealth between West and South and between West and East, in terms of income per head, are among the most important stimuli for migration. How far do they need to be reduced in order to reduce the migration pressure effectively?

Estimates for the years just before the revolutionary events in central and eastern Europe (Summers and Heston 1988) suggested that there was not that much of a difference between wealth levels in the South-West and the East of Europe. For instance Czechoslovakia was found to be on a par with Spain, and Hungary and Poland were in the same group as the lower income western countries like Portugal and Greece.

However, the disparities in Europe between East and West have since considerably increased. On the one hand, the West has seen modest but continuous growth. On the other hand, the East has seen a decline in GDP per head, due to the economic and political upheaval and the transition to a market economy that cut-off large sectors of the economy from their traditional markets.

The most recent Eurostat data on differences in GDP per head show a large variation between the income levels of the countries in central and eastern Europe. In the middle range are countries like Poland, Hungary, and Bulgaria, with income levels about a third of the average of the EU.[9] The ratio between the richest CEEC country (Slovenia) and the EU average is about one to two; whereas the ratio for the poorest country (Albania) and the EU average is as much as one to seven.

The countries of the southern and eastern banks of the Mediterranean show average income levels far below the average of the EU. This is no new phenomenon; development in these countries has always lagged considerably behind north western Europe. There is also a very large variance among the members of this group. Excluding countries like Libya (with oil revenues), the range goes from Morocco to Algeria, with the ratio to the EU average being 1:15 and 1:6 respectively.

Catch-up rhythms
On the basis of GDP figures, we may calculate the distance that has to be bridged in the catching-up process of the South and East. To calculate the likely speed of this process, we first assume that the mature economy of Western Europe will grow over the next decades at its historical long-term growth rate of some two to three per cent a year, (which implies a doubling over thirty years). We next assume, on the basis of the experience from the past and the present in the West, (see Molle and Van Mourik, 1988, 1989) that a difference of one third in wealth levels can be sustained without giving rise to large-scale migration.

The East is on average one third short of the EU mean of the target value; for instance, Poland is presently at two thirds of the EU mean. In order to catch up therefore, the eastern European countries have to realise, over a thirty-year period, average growth rates of four to seven per cent, depending on their starting position. Figures of around five per cent are realistic by historical standards, as witness the growth rates of the countries of southern Europe over the 1985–1992 period, in which they benefited significantly from Structural Fund aid. Such figures are also realistic by present records: the Czech Republic and Poland have growth rates of five to six per cent in 1995 and similar rates are forecast for the coming years.

The South is, on average, in a more disadvantaged position and their distance from the EU mean is quite large. Moreover, the record of these countries in terms of past growth rates is not very impressive. This may continue in the future, as their economies seem to be rather fragile with respect to the changes in competitiveness that are taking place in the world at the moment. Hence, one should reckon on very long catch-up periods between the South and West

Which factors need to be stimulated?

Additional growth can be realised by the countries of the two sending areas only by improving their performance in the major determinants of growth. The major factors are:

- *Inputs.* The supply of inputs can be differentiated further:

    For labour: total employment, hours worked, age and sex distribution of the workforce and education levels. Endogenous development of skills.

    For capital: investment in machinery, dwellings and international assets. Technical progress and productivity growth.

- *Markets.* A good access to markets creates the dynamic effects of enhanced competition, economies of scale, learning effects, and so on.

- *Infrastructure.* Productive investments are useless if they are not accompanied by complementary investments in infrastructure. Regional economists stress the need for good transport infrastructure, port and airport, road and rail, and for good telecommunications.

- *Governance.* The smooth functioning of the private sector depends critically on the existence of an efficient set of legal and administrative rules, absence of corruption and, the certainty of having court decisions executed. In general, this can be termed effective political organisation and administrative competence.

Many of the factors for growth cited here are actually complementary, so it is difficult to isolate the contribution of each of them.

Moreover the list is not stable over time; for instance, traditionally much emphasis has been given to natural resources, but recently the concern for sustainable development has drawn attention to the environmental consequences of such policies. Finally, the literature suggests that all these things are not of equal importance; the knowledge and the improvement of the quality of labour are among the most influential factors.

Aid programmes

General
Many of the countries of the Mediterranean and east European group score very poorly on the factors given above, and consequently their development is very slow. With the objective of helping these countries overcome these problems, governments have concluded bilateral agreements with them and international organisations have constructed multilateral programmes.

International aid is a transfer of resources on concessional terms. Much of it is Official Development Assistance, such as loans, given by official agencies with the objective of promoting the economic development and welfare of the recipient country, that have a grant element of at least 25 per cent (real cost compared to cost of market loans; see OECD, several years). Another important form of aid is technical co-operation, which covers assistance, nearly all in grants, for the improvement of the productive structure of the recipient country. In this framework come projects like education and training, the functioning of capital markets, industry and infrastructure, institutions and policy design.

Central and eastern Europe
Up until the events at the end of the 1980s, the countries of central and eastern Europe did not qualify for the status of developing country and so could not benefit from international aid. On the contrary, some of these countries were actually donors of aid (OECD, 1990). They did however receive some form of support, mostly in the form of loans; as a consequence some of the countries in the East have accumulated a very heavy external debt. For some countries this has been reduced and rescheduled so as to facilitate the transition of their economies.

Present aid programmes consist of components from national governments, from the EU, and from the international Aid Agencies. The PHARE and TACIS programmes of the EU which help the countries of the East, are by far the most important of these. But, not withstanding their considerable size (about 1.5 billion ECU a year), they fall far short of the demands of the East (20 billion ECU a year as a lower estimate, based on the experience of the EU with the Structural Funds). The demands of the South have not yet been quantified with a reasonable degree of accuracy; even taking into account factors such as their absorption capacity they are likely to far exceed the present level of one billion ECU a year. So in quantitative terms there is a big gap to be filled between the aid offered by the EU and the needs of the South and East.

In qualitative terms however, the present programmes seem to be rather well adapted to the needs of the recipient countries. They cover many of the areas identified earlier as determinants of growth: guarantees for private investments, support to labour and management training, to technology transfer; for transport and energy infrastructure; for telecommunication networks, for the cleaning up of environmental damage; and for advice on good governance, privatisation, systemic reform and policy design (see eg CEC 1993). Moreover, EU aid is available to help CEE countries that have to cope with macroeconomic stabilisation problems and has amounted to some five billion ECU over the past five years. (CEC1995a).

Mediterranean

The EU has had bi-lateral relations with the non-member countries of the Mediterranean area since the 1960s. They have been developed over the years, notably in the 1970s, when co-operation agreements were drawn up between the EU and the countries of the Southern and Eastern seaboard. Under these agreements, the EU and the beneficiary country drew up development programmes that were jointly financed by the government and the EU. The total amount of support that has in the past been made available in this way is estimated at some three billion ECU. One of the programmes dealt specifically with migration.

In recent years the need for a recasting of EU-Mediterranean relations has become manifest. It is in the interest of the EU to help the countries of the region with their stable development. To that end the MEDA scheme has recently been set up along the lines of the PHARE/TACIS programmes. The amount of money that has been made available is of the same order of magnitude (4.7 billion ECU for the period up to 1999).

The main objectives of the MEDA programme are to provide support to:

- economic transition in the beneficiary countries

- establishment of a Euro/Mediterranean free trade area, including private sector development, EU direct investments, upgrading of infrastructure

- the achievement of a better socio-economic balance, including eg rural activities, environment, human resources, social services

- regional and cross-border co-operation between the Mediterranean partners

The impact of aid on development

Aid is given to enhance the economic development of the beneficiary. But does it also have that effect?

Some say no or at least not enough. Their criticisms are: aid takes away the urgency for systemic reform; it decreases the savings ratio and increases consumption without improving the productive capacity; if used for the productive system it is often poorly oriented in technological and market terms; it benefits the donor more than the receiver; finally its objectives are unclear, so performance cannot be checked.

Others say yes: aid does work. By taking away bottlenecks to development, in capital provision, in infrastructure and in human capital formation, aid does contribute to economic performance. This is not to say that all aid has been positive, but that it has been positive on average. Its effectiveness critically depends on the specific form chosen and on the policies of the recipient countries. The latter point stresses the need for policy dialogue between donors and recipients.

South and East

Aid to central and eastern Europe is of very recent origin. Hence it is difficult to assess its impact. The studies that have been made on the degree to which the projects under the PHARE/TACIS programmes have indeed reached their specified targets do not permit one to come to any firm conclusions, the picture is too fragmented. Experience of the Netherlands Economic Institute (NEI) with the evaluation of all aid to one country (Romania) and to one sector in all beneficiary countries (finance) shows that most projects have contributed significantly to reaching the targets set. However, the absorption capacity of many countries is constrained by institutional factors at the central level. Projects involving local organisations (for instance in the realm of employment organisations and SMEs) tended to go well, as they were aloof from the problem of poor adaptation of central institutions.

West

We can also look at cases in the developed world to help illuminate the issue of aid and development. The aid programmes the EU executes in the framework of its cohesion policy are a case in point. They are designed to step up the economic growth in the member states that have to cope with either restructuring of old industrial sectors, or with backwardness in the development of a modern sector. They have a considerable size and impact. To give an example, the total amount of support from the structural funds given to countries like Portugal and Greece amounts to as much as two per cent of GDP and even seven per cent of total investment (CEC, 1995b).

EU structural funds are notably given to projects that improve the infrastructure (transport, energy, telecommunications), the quality of human resources (training, exchange), the innovativeness of firms. Several studies show that aid has been responsible for a significant part of the acceleration of growth that "Cohesion countries" have witnessed in the recent past. First, Marques-Mendes (1990) finds for the whole of the EU a positive effect of aid on the reduction of disparities and suggests that more aid would step up growth in the cohesion countries even further. Next, De la Fuente and Vives (1995) showed that public spending on infrastructure and education in the backward regions of Spain had speeded up growth in these regions by two per cent. Finally, Bradley *et al* (1995) show, with the help of a macro model, that European aid has resulted in an initial acceleration of one per cent in the growth of GDP per head of Ireland: after some years the growth bonus of EU aid becomes much higher, as supply side effects need time to materialise.

This overall positive conclusion does not mean that all aid is effective, nor does it deny that the efficiency of aid could not be stepped up. Indeed, a reform of the EU system to concentrate efforts on the regions that qualify most for aid, would in general have positive effects (Molle 1996).

Conclusions

On the basis of this preliminary evaluation one can conclude that:

- Aid programmes towards structural improvement are on average effective.

- Aid to eastern Europe needs to be gradually stepped up to at some 30 to 40 billion ECU a year, in order to attain a convergence of GDP levels at around 2020 that practically eliminates the impetus for mass-migration from East to West in the, by then, integrated area of the enlarged EU.

- Aid will be ineffective if it is not set in a framework of integration of goods, services and capital markets for both South and East.

- Aid has to be set in the framework of systemic reform. In the East this implies adapting the institutions to fit the EU set-up. In the South it implies structural adaptation of their economies to a system that is open to the world market.

Specific policies for the labour market and for education

The role of markets and of government

The countries of central and eastern Europe are still in a process of transition from a centrally planned economy to a market economy. The countries of the southern and eastern bank of the Mediterranean basin have to cope with structural adaptation involving a reduction of the considerable intervention of the state in the economy. Under such circumstances markets do not function in an efficient way. This applies in particular to labour markets.

We may take as an example the improvement of skills through training. The theory of how training can reduce migration is as follows: training has an upward effect on productivity so decreasing unit labour costs and product prices, and resulting in a growing product demand and output, an increased income per head and hence a decreased incentive to migrate. However, if the new supply of trained workers does not find employment, because markets are not working well enough in terms of flexibility, training will not have any real impact. In that case, providing aid to skill formation in the form of training may even have an adverse effect on migration; well-trained unemployed will have an even greater incentive to seize the opportunities in the western European countries.

This illustrates that making markets more efficient is an essential precondition for a growth stimulating policy that reduces the potential for migration. As to the labour-market this means:

- Companies should be submitted to market rule (through a programme of privatisation). There should be incentives to keep down internal labour reserves to a minimum level.

- Wages should be negotiated freely; companies and workers should have the freedom to deviate from collective bargaining results. It is very important that wages can move freely, so that there is some tendency towards equilibrium in the labour market.

- Information on supply and demand on the labour market should be exchanged. Labour offices have an important task in collecting information about vacancies and unemployed persons and matching the two.

- Social security has to be kept at a level that means workers accept jobs at wage levels that are realistic in the context of Eastern and Southern economies. In addition, an over generous social security system would inevitably lead to a discrepancy between gross and net wages, favouring growth in the informal economy.

We should be clear however, that making markets work more efficiently does not mean a policy of laissez-faire. Markets will never function perfectly by nature. This is especially true of the labour market and the market for education. So long-term policy must include the designing of a new role for the government to cope with the imperfections of markets.

Foreign aid can and should be directed to the creating of efficient labour markets and to designing forms of government intervention in education and training that improve allocational efficiency.

Education

The market for education suffers from a number of imperfections, which would lead to a severe under-investment in training and education if the government and the social partners would not intervene.

The imperfections are a result of :

- the special character of education, some of its value not being reflected in a market price

- the uncertainty of the return on training and education and the impossibility of insuring the risks involved

- the free rider problem

Under-investment is likely to occur most in sectors with a highly mobile labour force, a strong sensitivity to cyclical and seasonal fluctuations and a highly competitive output market.

Educational policy should be directed to both initial education and adult education. It is very important that the educational and training system is connected to the labour market. Schools, training institutions and students must have incentives to choose the kind of courses that are wanted by employers. Employers should play an important role in vocational education and training.

Foreign aid can finance part of the cost of education. Experience has shown that the effectiveness of financial support is highest where subsidies to training institutions, students and companies are made specific for certain professions, groups and types of companies rather than are general.

Other relevant items for educational policy are:

- Adaptation of the curricula to the new demands on the labour market. The service sector, including activities such as trade, commerce, transport, communication and finance, demand labour with more knowledge of foreign (western) languages, business administration, banking and finance and accounting.

- More attention to general formation in primary and the first level of secondary education. In view of the development towards a (social) market economy where entrepreneurship is important, relevant items are creativity, flexibility, initiative and self-reliance. Also the choice and orientation of careers needs attention. A way to establish this might be education on the basis of projects and through more self-education, with the teacher in the role of mentor.

International integration may lead towards a coupling of training with foreign direct investment. The latter will introduce new technology and employees have to be able to adapt to. They may acquire the necessary skills either at home or in the "mother" company in one of the western countries. The latter variant, involving temporary migration, has a number of advantages:

- lower vacancy-problems in the western countries, thereby reducing the demand for (illegal) labour

- lower spontaneous labour migration

- increased human capital in the East and South, not only by raising skills and experience, but also by increasing knowledge of the workings of market organisations

To let the scheme work successfully some conditions have to be fulfilled. In the first place return to the country of origin must be assured, for instance through financial stimuli. The company has to take some responsibility for this. Second, participants have to be selected from the group of potential emigrants, otherwise it might only lead to a rise in (temporary) migration. Experience with this type of schemes is very good (see for instance the Hungarian case reported by Nagy in OECD 1994).

Labour market
Unemployment and unfilled demand are persistent characteristics of labour markets in market economies. It is important to note that in capitalist societies government intervention in the labour market was caused by the incidence of unemployment rather than vice versa.

Modern labour market theory has come up with a number of explanations for the unemployment phenomenon. First, labour economists have stressed the fact that information about job opportunities and people searching for jobs is not costless, implying positive unemployment and vacancies. Second, due to turnover costs workers have a certain amount of monopoly power, setting wages above the market clearing level. Third, individual productivity is an unobserved quantity so that companies will have to set wages above the market clearing level in order to keep productivity at a sufficient level. Finally, social security and legal constraints with respect to things like lay-offs and hours, can cause inflexibility.

Modern theory not only explains why unemployment prevails, but also, to some extent, why some groups are more liable to unemployment than others. They also give a theoretical justification for an active labour market policy to promote an efficient matching of demand and supply and to ensure more equal chances of employment for different groups. In most countries an employment organisation exists, managed by the government and/or the social partners that assumes the responsibility for the development and implementation of labour market policy.

The following instruments are used:

- active matching of vacancies and unemployed persons.

- providing information about the actual labour market situation and future prospects.

- testing and advising with respect to occupational choice.

- employment and training schemes for the disadvantaged

- regular training in order to solve bottlenecks on the labour market

Most of these instruments, especially the first two and the last one, have a clear economic function. Some (the last two) have an overlap with education policy. The forth one belongs to the realm of social policy.

To prepare the labour offices in the partner countries of the EU in the East and the South for their new role, projects aimed at increasing the experience and expertise of their staff should be favoured by international aid programmes. Part of their skills should be to evaluate the type of demands that will be induced by foreign direct investment. To that end some knowledge about regional comparative advantages and location factors is needed. The relevant factors are quite different for different regions, so the responsibility for the policy needs to be decentralised as well.

Conclusions
We have seen then that those elements are needed for successful policies to ensure the labour

Governments should create the conditions for the efficient functioning of markets. This is however not sufficient; the nature of these markets requires some form of government intervention to increase allocational efficiency.

Foreign aid should be used to increase the financial capacity to set up education and training projects. The better the supply of new skills is geared to the specific demands on the local labour market, the higher the effectiveness of the projects.

Labour offices can make an important contribution to the efficient functioning of the labour market. Aid to this form of institutional development can provide the necessary competences for the staff to make these offices operate effectively.

Encouragingly the proposed policies fit actual international aid programmes rather well. Projects and programmes on labour market issues and education are part of the aid PHARE, TACIS and MEDA give to economic reform.

Final remarks

We have tried to see in how far migration towards the EU can be decreased by increasing foreign aid from the EU both with respect to the countries of central and eastern Europe on the one hand and those of the southern and eastern shores of the Mediterranean sea on the other hand.

It has been made clear that reducing migration is a desirable goal for all parties. Because the young, well-educated and active people have a high incentive to leave, it is likely that mass-migration will reduce the human capital stock in the eastern and southern countries to a considerable extent. Mass-migration is not very helpful to the western countries either, because they are already confronted with unemployment, and considerable difficulties of integration of earlier immigrants.

Although policy measures in the western countries can reduce migration to some extent, the real solution to the problem in the long term is the creation of jobs and the improvement of living standards in the eastern and southern countries. Policy should be oriented to stimulating long-term growth, taking the short-term migration problems into account. Market access policies are very important in this respect.

Any change in the push and pull factors that determine migration will take some time to take effect. However, structural aid, and in particular aid to education and training that improves the performance of the labour, can help to improve the situation in both eastern and southern countries. Better job opportunities and higher wages in the countries of the East and the South diminish the wage difference between sending and recipient countries and hence the impetus to migration.

Are the suggested policies sufficient? Can they induce employment and income growth to such an extent that most people are encouraged to stay? On the basis of our analysis it is not yet possible to give a definite answer to this question. Over the coming years experiments with the practical implementation of policy measures will show in what ways the composition and the scope of the policies need to be adjusted in order to obtain the desired effects.

Endnotes

1 The present paper draws heavily on Molle, de Koning and Zandvliet (1992)
2 For reasons of convenience we will call the different areas West, East and South respectively. The West should be more accurately termed the North and West
3 The information on the Polish migration confirms this picture; in the 1980s emigration absorbed nearly the entire increase in the population of working age, while the size of the younger segment of the potential labour force declined. The brain-drain was also obvious; for instance the number of tertiary educated emigrants was identical to the number of university graduates. For physicians and engineers it was even higher (Okólski, 1991). From the scarce information on emigration from other eastern European countries it appears that the characteristics of the migrants are similar to those for Poland. There is no information on the occupational structure of the migration.
4 There are some indications that under the new circumstances – where it is now easier to leave and return to the eastern European countries – the group that resides temporarily in the West is growing. But an exact distinction is difficult to make, because a lot of the temporary stays last longer than a few years (Okólski, 1991).
5 Eg in the Netherlands 43 per cent for immigrants and 11 per cent of the Dutch population were unemployed in 1994.
6 Okólski (1991) mentions the "double-life" aspects of the illegal migrant: hard work in the West vs. spurious work in the home country, discrimination vs. preference, living and working in humiliating conditions vs. displaying "millionaire" manners, etc.
7 According to the European legislation non-EC employees can be employed only when labour with the demanded qualifications cannot be hired either in the home country, or in one of the other member-countries.
8 Illegal employment does not necessarily go hand in hand with illegal payment; often taxes and social security payments are payed by the employer. Whenever this does not happen exploitation of labour takes place. Much depends on the magnitude of the mentioned motives (generally speaking the stronger the vacancy-motive the lesser the extent in which illegal payment takes place). The illegal worker is not always directly employed by the employer; there are strong indications that a large part of the irregular employed work as hired labourers and through labour brokers. This fits the need for flexibility on the side of the employers.
9 Measured in PPP.

References

Borjas J (1995) The economic benefits of immigration, *Journal of Economic Perspectives*. Vol 9.2.

Bradley J, O'Donell N, Sheridan N & Whelan K (1995). *Regional aid and convergence, Evaluating the impact of the structural funds on the European Periphery*, Avebury, Aldershot.

CEC (1993) Shaping a market economy legal system, (law reform in the independent states), *European Economy*. no 2, Brussels/Luxembourg.

CEC (1994) The economic interpenetration between the European Union and Eastern Europe, *European Economy*, Reports and Studies, no 6, Brussels/Luxembourg.

CEC (1995a) Implementation of macro financial assistance to third countries in 1994, *European Economy*, Reports and studies, no 2 Brussels/Luxembourg.

CEC (1995b) *Competitiveness and the regions, fifth periodic report on the social and economic situation and development of the regions in the Community*, Brussels/Luxemburg.

Friedberg RM & Hunt J (1995) The impact of immigrants on host country wages, employment and growth, *Journal of Economic Perspectives*, Vol 9.2.

Fuente A. de la & Vives X (1995) Infrastructure and education as instruments of regional policy; evidence from Spain, *Economic Policy*, Vol 20.

Keely CB & Tran BN (1989) Remittance from labor migration: evaluations, performance and implications, *International Migration Review*, Vol 13, no. 3.

Lindbeck A (1991) *Microfoundations of unemployment theory*, Paper for the EALE Conference, Madrid.

Marques-Mendes AJ (1990) Economic cohesion in Europe; the impact of the Delors Plan, *Journal of Common Market Studies*, Vol 29.

Molle WTM (1994) *Economics of European integration; theory, practice, policy*, Dartmouth, Aldershot, 2nd edition.

Molle WTM (1996) *Economic integration and cohesion policies; the pan-European experience*, EUR/NEI, Rotterdam

Molle WTM, Koning J de & Zandvliet C (1992) *Can foreign aid reduce East West migration in Europe? With special reference to Poland*. ILO working papers, MIG/WP67, Geneva; published later as WR Böhming and ML Schloeter Paredes (1994) (eds), Aid in place of migration, ILO, Geneva.

Molle WTM & Mourik A van (1988) International movements of labour under conditions of economic integration, the case of Western Europe, *Journal of Common Market Studies*, Vol 26.3.

Molle WTM & Mourik A van (1989) *Wage differentials in the European Community*, Avebury, Aldershot.

Molle WTM & Zandvliet C (1994) South North immigration in the Western European countries, the case of France, the UK, and the Netherlands, in H Siebert (ed) (1994) *Migration, a challenge for Europe*, Mohr, Tübingen, pp 85-115.

OECD (several years) *Development Cooperation*, Paris (annual aid statistics).

OECD (1994) *Migration and Development, new partnerships for cooperation*, Paris.

Okólski M (1991) *Migratory movements from countries of Central and Eastern Europe*, paper for the Conference of Ministers on the movement of persons coming from Central and Eastern European countries, Vienna, 24-25 January 1991, ed. Council of Europe, Strasbourg.

Rettab B (1996) *The economic performance of the immigrant work force: a case study of Moroccans in the Netherlands*, Erasmus University Rotterdam (EUR), the Netherlands.

Siebert H (ed) (1994) *Migration, a challenge for Europe*, Mohr, Tübingen.

Spencer S (ed) (1994) *Immigration as an economic asset; the German experience*, IPPR/Trentham Books, London

Summers R & Heston A (1988) A new set of international comparisons of real product and prices. estimates for 130 countries; 1950-1985, *Review of income and wealth*, Vol 34.

Zandvliet C & Gravensteijn-Ligthelm J (1994). *Illegale arbeid, omvang en effecten*, Ministerie van Sociale Zaken, Den Haag.

Zimmermann KF (1995) Tackling the European Migration Problem, *Journal of Economic Perspectives*, Vol 9.2.

5. Economic developments within the EU: the role of population movements[1]
John Salt

Introduction

There is no doubt that in recent years international migration has held an unusually high place on the European political agenda. The "will they, won't they come" guessing games of the immediate aftermath of 1989 generated enormous heat in the continent's chancelleries and Parliaments, although there was not often much illumination. Seven years on, we know a lot more than we did, and the debate has shifted subtly in a number of ways. The prospect of a lot of new migrants led to a second look at the degree to which those already arrived had been integrated. Asylum became the prominent issue. Politically, the trend has been strongly towards harmonisation of entry and other migration policies.

The aim of this chapter is predominantly empirical. It begins by reviewing the extent to which the free movement provisions of the succession of treaties that now comprise the Treaty of Union have resulted in more migration. It then goes on to outline the main trends in the 1990s in migrant stocks and flows. Finally it focuses on one group, the highly skilled, widely regarded as a critical element in the engine of economic growth.

The EU as an area of free movement

From its very beginning the European Community was more than a free trade area, having the additional aim of fostering and encouraging a "political" community. What better way to achieve this than some form of common "citizenship" an essential element of which was the right of free movement? By 1968 a customs union, together with a common external tariff, was in place, and the two were accompanied by generally unfettered movement of EC nationals with the right to live and work in other member states.

The next step was to create a real common market, comprising four freedoms: those of goods, services, capital and labour. The 1986 Single

European Act included abolition of border controls for persons, and the extension of freedom of movement (eg by the unemployed, Third Country Nationals (TCNs), and through the mutual recognition of qualifications).

Despite these free movement provisions the evidence shows clearly that migration did not increase much within the EU. Most increases in migration were by Third Country Nationals (TCNs). In the 1960s, fears of an Italian "flood" (an early use of aquatic imagery) proved false. In the 1970s the entry of the UK, Ireland and Denmark into the EU did not prompt a wave of migration, nor did that of Greece in the 1980s. So far there is little evidence that this pattern will be broken in the 1990s by Spain and Portugal. The only exception to this is that Portuguese immigration into France increased sharply during 1993, suggesting that where there is already a large established minority, chain migration effects may hold sway. By the same token, there is no reason to believe that the membership of Sweden, Finland and Austria will lead to any noticeable increase in migration between EU members.

The data on the stocks of foreign population and employees in member states show that since the 1970s the numbers of foreigners who were other EU nationals has largely stagnated (Denmark, Ireland, Luxembourg, Netherlands, Portugal) or fallen (Belgium, France, Germany). Only Greece and Spain, where the statistics are unreliable, and the UK (where the situation is complicated by the immigration of the Irish) show increases. In contrast, trends in immigration by TCNs have been strongly upward.

Why didn't more movement occur?
It would appear that the main reason migration did not increase was that increased trade occurred instead. Between 1960 and 1992 trade between the founder states increased from 35 to 60 per cent of all their trade. Statistics show consistently that intra-EC trade has grown much faster than trade with the rest of the world (Werner, 1995). So intra-EC/EU trade has grown while intra-EC/EU migration has not.

With this growth in trade has come economic convergence. Werner's analysis shows that between 1960 and 1993 the standard deviation between levels of national GDP per head fell while major regional differences in GDP between regions have been tackled to a degree with a succession of regional and structural funds. There has, therefore, been a falling economic gradient between countries.

Table 5.1: Stock of foreign population in selected western European Countries 1980-1994 (thousands)[1]

	1980	1982	1984	1986	1988	1990	1992	1994[18]
AUSTRIA[2]	282.7	302.9	297.8	314.9	344.0	456.1	623.0	713.5
BELGIUM[3]	-	891.2	897.6	853.2	868.8	904.5	909.3	922.3
DENMARK[4]	101.6	103.1	107.7	128.3	142.0	160.6	180.1	196.7
FINLAND[5]	12.8	14.3	16.8	17.3	18.7	26.3	40.8	62.0
FRANCE[6]	-	3714.2	-	-	-	3607.6	-	-
GERMANY[7]	4453.3	4666.9	4363.7	4512.7	4489.1	5241.8	6495.8	6990.5
GREECE[8]	213.0	229.7	234.1	220.1	222.6	229.1	262.3	244.0
IRELAND[9,13]	-	-	-	-	-	27.6	-	-
ITALY[10]	298.7	358.9	403.9	450.2	645.4	781.1	925.2	922.7
LUXEMBOURG[17]	94.3	95.6	96.9	96.8	100.9	110.0	119.7	130.0
NETHERLANDS	520.9	546.5	558.7	568.0	623.7	692.4	757.4	774.2
NORWAY[11]	82.6	90.6	97.8	109.3	135.9	143.3	154.0	164.0
PORTUGAL[12,13]	49.3	57.7	72.6	87.0	94.7	107.8	121.5	157.1
SPAIN[13]	182.0	200.9	226.5	293.2	360.0	407.7	393.1	-
SWEDEN[14]	421.7	405.5	390.6	390.8	421.0	483.7	499.1	537.4
SWITZERLAND[15]	892.8	925.8	932.4	956.0	1006.5	1100.3	1213.5	1300.1
UK[16]	-	-	1601.0	1820.0	1821.0	1875.0	1985.0	2032.0

Sources and notes

1. Data as of 31/12 of year indicated extracted, except for France, UK and otherwise indicated, from population registers.
2. 1983 to 1993 data from OECD (1995)
3. In 1985, as a consequence of a modification of the nationality code, some persons who formerly would have been counted as foreigners were included as nationals. This led to a marked decrease in the foreign population. Eurostat (1995) and OECD (1995)
4. Eurostat (1994) and OECD (1995)
5. Central statistical office of Finland.
6. Population censuses on 4/3/82 and 6/3/90. The figure for the census of 20/2/75 is 3442.4.
7. Data as of 30/10 up to 1984 and in 1990 and as of 31/12 for all other years. Except for 1991 & 1992, refers to western Germany. FSO.
8. National Statistical Service of Greece (1994) and Ministry of Public Order in 1995 report to the OECD by the Greek SOPEMI Correspondent. 1993 and 1994 figures rounded.
9. Department of Justice, annual returns, (excludes U.K. citizens).
10. Data are adjusted to take account of the regularisations which occurred in 1987-88 and 1990. The fall in numbers for 1989 results from a review of the foreigners' register (removing duplicate registrations, accounting for returns). Source: Ministry of the Interior, elaborated by CENSIS.
11. From 1987, asylum seekers whose requests are being processed are included. Numbers for earlier years were fairly small.
12. Serviço de Estrangeiros e Fronteiras. 1993 figure includes estimated 39,200 from special regularisation.
13. Eurostat (1994) and Sopemi (1994)
14. Some foreigners permits of short duration are not counted (mainly citizens of other Nordic countries).
15. Numbers of foreigners with annual residence permits (including, up to 31/12/82, holders of permits of durations below 12 months) and holders of settlement permits (permanent permits). Seasonal and frontier workers are excluded. 1993 data from Sopemi. 1994 figure taken in April.
16. Numbers estimated from the annual labour force survey.
17. Provisonal estimate for 1994 figure.
18. 1994 figures from Central Statistical Offices etc. in the 1995 reports to the OECD by the individual country SOPEMI Correspondents.

The broader picture: trends in the foreign population in Europe

Stocks

In western Europe as a whole, stocks of foreign population have increased considerably in recent years (Table 5.1). In 1993-4 or thereabouts (using the latest date for which statistics are available) there were around 19.2 million foreign nationals resident in western Europe, with perhaps a further quarter of a million or so in eastern Europe. In 1988 (1989 for Ireland and 1990 for France), the figure stood at about 14.93 million. Hence, from 1988 to 1994 total foreign national stocks in western Europe increased by about 4.27 million (28.6 per cent), However, in recent years there seems to have been a noticeable fall in the rate of increase.

It is more difficult to obtain accurate and comparable data across Europe for stocks of labour than for the foreign population as a whole. There are problems of knowing who is included, and which sources might be used. In addition, unrecorded workers are almost certainly proportionately more important in the labour market than are unrecorded residents in the total population.

The evidence from Table 5.2 suggests that in western Europe in 1993-4 (using the latest data for each country) there were about 8.6 million recorded foreign workers. This represents an increase of about 39 per cent on the 1988 figure (6.2 million). Over this period the western European economy has experienced both slowing growth, the re-unification of Germany and the recession of the early 1990s. A longer term perspective may be had by comparing the situation in 1980, 1988 and 1994 for those seven countries in Table 5.2 for which data are available throughout. In 1980 these countries had 4.55 million foreign workers, but by 1988 this total had fallen slightly to 4.5 million (-1.1 per cent); in 1994 (1993 where no figure is available for 1994) the number had risen to 5.23 million, an increase in six years of three-quarters of a million (16 per cent). For these countries, therefore, all of the increase in the foreign labour force since 1980 occurred after 1988.

Any attempt at producing comparative tables of the migration situation across the countries of Europe is fraught with difficulties (see, for example, Salt, Singleton and Hogarth, 1994). The analysis that follows must therefore be treated with caution, since the definitions and concepts used in data collection differ from country to country. The aggregate figures reported here are best thought of as indicative rather than definitive.

Table 5.2: Stocks of foreign labour in selected western European Countries, 1980-1994[1] (thousands)

	1980	1982	1984	1986	1988	1990	1992	1994
AUSTRIA[2,18]	174.7	156.0	138.7	146.0	150.9	217.6	273.9	291.0
BELGIUM[3,18]	-	-	182.5	179.2	179.4	-	-	-
DENMARK[4,18]	-	-	53.6	60.1	65.1	68.8	74.0	-
FINLAND[5,18]	4.5	5.3	6.0	6.4	8.0	13.0	14.7	-
FRANCE[6]	1458.2	1503.0	1658.2	1555.7	1557.0	1549.5	1517.8	1593.9
GERMANY[7,18]	2015.6	1785.5	1608.1	1600.2	1656.0	1837.7	2103.9	2168.0
GREECE[8,18]	-	-	-	-	23.9	23.2	33.1	26.2
IRELAND[9]	-	-	-	-	21.5	21.3	-	-
ITALY[10]	-	-	-	-	187.8	380.9	507.5	474.6
LUXEMBG[11,18]	51.9	52.3	53.0	58.7	69.4	84.7	98.2	60.2
NETHERLS[12,18]	188.1	185.2	168.8	169.0	176.0	197.0	229.0	216.0
NORWAY[13]	-	-	-	-	49.5	46.3	46.6	-
PORTUGAL[8,18]	-	-	-	-	35.2	36.9	59.2	77.6
SPAIN[14]	-	-	-	-	58.2	85.4	139.4	-
SWEDEN[15,18]	234.1	227.7	219.2	214.9	220.2	246.0	233.0	213.0
SWITZERLD[16,18]	501.2	526.2	539.3	566.9	607.8	669.8	716.7	740.3
UK[17]	-	-	744.0	815.0	871.0	882.0	902.0	864.0

Sources and notes

1. Includes the unemployed, except in Benelux and the U.K. Frontier and seasonal workers are excluded unless otherwise stated.
2. Annual average. Work permits delivered plus permits still valid. Figures may be over-estimated because some persons hold more than one permit. Self-employed are excluded. Data for 1990 and 1991 have been adjusted to correct for a temporary over-issue of work permits relative to the number of jobs held by foreigners, between August 1990 and June 1991.
3. Excludes the unemployed and self-employed.
4. Data from population registers and give the count as of the end of November each year except December (end of December). Source: Sopemi Annual Report, OECD (1995)
5. Estimate, assuming activity rates of the 1980s (slightly under 50 per cent).
6. Data as of March each year derived from the labour force survey.
7. Data as of 30 September each year. Includes frontier workers but not the self-employed. Refers to western Germany.
8. Excludes the unemployed, Eurostat.
9. 991 data excludes the unemployed, LFS.
10. 1994 figure to 31/8/94. Source: CENSIS
11. Data as of 1 October each year. Foreigners in employment, including aprentices, trainees and frontier workers. Excludes the unemployed.
12. Estimates as of 31 March, including frontier workers, but excluding the self-employed and their family members as well as the unemployed.
13. Excludes unemployed. Data are for the second quarter Source: Sopemi Annual Report (1995).
14. Data derived from the annual labour force survey.
15. Statistics Sweden, LFS. 1990-92 data corrected.
16. Data as of 31 December each year. Numbers of foreigners with annual residence permits (including up to 31 December 1982, holders of permits of durations below 12 months) and holders of settlement permits (permanent permits) who engage in gainful activity.
17. Excludes the unemployed.
18. Additional source: Central Statisical Offices etc, in the 1995 reports to the OECD by the individual country SOPEMI Correspondents.

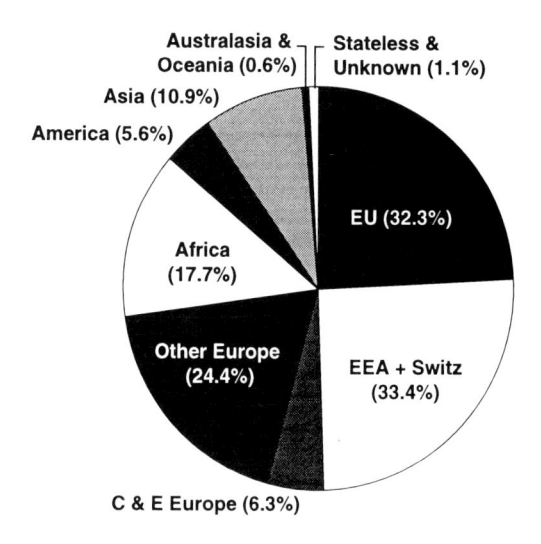

Fig. 5.1: Foreign populations in the EU (as at 1.1.93)
Source: Eurostat (1995)

How many Third Country Nationals might be eligible for free movement?
There were 16.9 million foreign nationals resident in EU states at the beginning of 1993 (Fig.5.1 and Annexe 5.1). Almost 5.5 million of these (32.3 per cent) were nationals of other member states. The inclusion of the EEA states plus Switzerland brings this total to 5.7 million, 33 per cent of all foreigners in the EU. A further 4.1 million (24.4 per cent) were from Other Europe (mainly Yugoslavs and Turks). Africans totalled three million (17.7 per cent), Asians 1.9 million (10.9 per cent). central and eastern Europe, including the former Soviet Union, accounted for about a million of the EU's foreign stock, only 6.3 per cent of the total. However, this figure represents those officially registered in the statistics: many temporary migrants from the east are not included.

The origins of foreign migrants in western Europe are diverse. In Luxembourg, Ireland, and Belgium, over half of the foreign population is from other EU countries; for Spain, UK and France the proportion is a third. Two-thirds of Switzerland's (not an EEA country) foreign nationals are EU citizens. For most countries, however, the bulk of their foreign national population comes from outside the EEA.

The pattern of foreign nationals in EU countries reflects a complex set of geographical locations and migration histories. In the case of the UK, Ireland and Spain proximity to a fellow EU member, together with a long history of population interchange, is clearly important (although this is not the case for Portugal as a destination). The situation in Belgium and Luxembourg reflects their geographical location, surrounded as they are by larger EU neighbours with open borders.

The significance of other regions as sources of foreign migrants varies with destination country. Africa is a particularly important source for France and Portugal reflecting earlier colonial ventures, and for Italy and Belgium to a lesser extent. America is important for Portugal and Spain (mainly South America), and also for Greece and Italy. Asia is a major source for the UK, Greece and Italy, though for different reasons and with emphases on different parts of that large and diverse continent. The UK receives Asian immigrants mainly from the Indian sub-continent, largely for settlement purposes. Italy receives mainly from South East Asia (particularly Filipinos), Greece from proximate countries in the Middle East region.

The dominance of Germany as a destination for foreign nationals from non-EU European countries is also clear: it received over a quarter of EEA (plus Switzerland) foreigners, and almost two-thirds of those from Central and Eastern Europe and from Other Europe. Germany's Asian numbers are enhanced by Vietnamese nationals recruited to the former GDR. However, African nationals in Germany are comparatively few. Despite the links between Spain and Portugal and the Americas, the UK receives the largest proportion of foreign nationals from that continent (mainly the US) and, not surprisingly, about seven in ten of those from Australasia and Oceania.

There is little reason to believe that substantial numbers of these people would move to another EU country if given the right to do so, mainly because the nature of their migration into Europe has been historically determined by colonial relationships, the presence of their countrymen in the host countries and so on.

Flows

For those countries for which it is possible to calculate net flows the period 1983–c1994 saw a net aggregate gain of 7.2 million by migration, including about three-quarters of a million in 1992–93 (see Annexe 5.2). From the mid-1980s the data suggest that there have been net gains for most countries, but that recently net gains have tended to fall, almost universally in those countries for which data are available. However, these data probably underestimate total net inflows, since for the most part they exclude asylum seekers and some categories of temporary immigrants, many of whom it is known stay illegally.

Nevertheless, there is solid evidence that recorded immigration trends are now downwards, suggesting that stricter and more harmonised entry controls are working.

The story on total population flows is echoed by inflows of labour, with steady increases in most countries until the early 1990s. Since then there has been a general downturn in labour inflows for those countries for which data are available. The statistics underestimate total flows.[2]

"Unrecorded" movements
Some attempts have been made to try and assess the scale of illegal immigration, using data from border control authorities on apprehensions, illegal trespassing, detentions etc. (ICMPD, 1994). The estimates suggest that irregular (asylum, displaced and illegals) inflows have continued to increase, from about 20 per cent of total flows in 1985 to 37 per cent in 1993. By 1993 illegal inflows in western Europe were estimated at 350,000, considerably higher than a few years before. In total, about 60,000 aliens were apprehended in 1993 at the borders of countries in eastern, central and western Europe, on their way to countries in western Europe; perhaps four to six times more managed to pass freely through the green borders to their country of destination (Widgren, 1994).

A changing relationship between supply and demand?

If we go back to the 1950s and 1960s, the *gastarbeiter* era was characterised by a high level of demand for labour in western Europe. The situation today is different, and suggests that there is likely to be little demand for much new labour immigration. Indeed, it would appear that today the main engine for immigration into western Europe is driving push factors in the emigration countries.

There has been fundamental sectoral and technological restructuring of economies, resulting in major changes in the labour market. Gone are the Fordist manufacturing industries, replaced in part by low level, labour intensive service employment. All governments have imposed constraints of various kinds on opening up their labour markets. Measures include minimum rates of pay and conditions, health and safety regulations and social security benefits.

There is an abundance of existing supply, with perhaps 20 million unemployed, of whom over a quarter are aged under 25. To these may be added a reservoir of married women who would take work, by one calculation totalling up to 30 million. Hence, there is an unused supply of about 50 million indigenous labour (Coleman, 1992). In any case, the so-called demographic gap cannot effectively be dealt with by immigration. The consequence would be unsustainable levels of immigration and integration.

On the supply side, the situation is mixed. Unlike the countries of the South, Eastern Europe is not faced with demographic pressure for emigration. Furthermore, the introduction of democracy has reduced the political reasons for emigration, thus encouraging people to stay. The major exceptions are in the eastern and southern parts of the former Soviet Union, but there is little evidence at the moment that emigration from here to Western Europe will occur.

Nevertheless, the economic situation in the former Warsaw Pact region remains weak and will encourage some emigration, which may in turn lead to a self-feeding process of migration. The weakness stems from the existence of agricultural over-employment, manufacturing monoliths, and a weak service sector. All create emigration pressures in the short and medium terms. Many of these movements have been very ephemeral in nature, labour tourism, petty trading and the like. Short-term solutions have been new *gastarbeiter*-type programmes, mainly German, involving a quarter of a million people at most.

In the countries of the South it is different. It is a commonly held view that rising population in Third World countries, coupled with ever-widening economic disparities between North and South, will create irresistible pressures for emigration from poor countries. Increasing restrictions on entry in European countries are largely predicated on this view. Furthermore, political and growing environmental uncertainties in the South, leading to more asylum seeking and "environmental refugeeism", merely add grist to the fortress Europe mill.

A number of studies have called attention to differences in the rates of population growth between Europe and its migrant origins in developing countries, compounded by comparative age structures. In most European countries, the ageing process is well under way, in sharp contrast to the situation in the countries of the South: for example, the Mediterranean basin has the steepest demographic gradient in the world.

Potential demographic pressures in some origin countries are exacerbated by weak economic performances. There is little chance of the urban economies of the countries of the South being able to cope with the large number of people who will move to them from rural areas as well as their own natural increment. The frustrated expectations of an internally migrant population may then be channelled into a desire to move overseas. However, the processes by which this may come about are as yet little known.

In addition to their disadvantages in demography (growth too fast) and economy (growth too slow), many countries of the South, and particularly those of North Africa, are vulnerable environmentally. Droughts in Africa during the 1980s, with large fluctuations from year to year, combine with fears of the consequences of global warming to suggest that emigration of "environmental refugees" is a distinct possibility.

To these disadvantages at home should be added the gains derived from emigration in the form of remittances and savings. These total around US$70 billion per annum (Russell and Teitelbaum, 1992). To national governments they are an economic lifeline, accounting in some cases for over half of their import bills. For individual households they play a fundamental role in their survival strategies.

The new movement of expertise

There has been a growing recognition of the importance of international recruitment and movement by the highly skilled. The core of the interest is economic. Modern industries and services increasingly rely upon the acquisition, deployment and use of human expertise to add value in their operations. Where this expertise is not available locally, employers frequently search for it abroad. They do this in a number of ways: direct recruitment from the external labour market; from within their own corporate internal labour markets; by acquiring businesses overseas; through partnership agreements or joint ventures; or from specialist firms. Frequently this movement is relatively short-term, and takes the form of a secondment or limited period assignment, perhaps for two or three years only. The consequence is that the economically most developed countries routinely exchange high level skills, while increasingly the less developed world is being brought into skill exchange and 'brain drain' networks.

Corporate relocation is a major element in the movement of highly skilled labour. According to the Labour Force Survey (unpublished), during the period 1985–95, 261,000 workers were transferred by their employers into the UK, an average of 24,000 per annum. Half were UK citizens, half were foreigners. We can use these figures to make some estimate of the total amount of international corporate relocation involving the UK labour market. Let us assume that the 12,000 Britons are returning from secondment abroad, and that the 12,000 foreign nationals are coming to work in the UK for UK and non-UK owned organisations. Further, let us assume that the average secondment period is two years (empirical research with large organisations has shown this to be a reasonable assumption). Assuming that in any one year 12,000 Britons go out, and the same number return it would seem that annually around 24,000 Britons are in an expatriate situation within corporate international labour markets. About 12,000 foreign nationals come in each year, and a similar number leave after their two year secondment. On this basis, the annual total number of corporate transferees involving companies in the UK would be about 48,000.

Perhaps the best indicator of the value placed on international professional, managerial and technical (PMT) workers is the amount employers are prepared to invest in their relocation. One recent study (Salt, Mervin and Shortland, 1993) estimated that the average net overseas cost per executive was about £87,500 per year. On this estimate, TNCs in the UK are spending about £4.2 billion (US$6.3 billion) per year on moving their highly skilled staff. The enormous cost of relocation, however, suggests that employers are under continuing pressure to consider other, less expensive, ways of moving skills internationally.

What is at issue now is how far this process of mobilising the highly skilled internationally is likely to go. There is some evidence to suggest that for a number of reasons, particularly monetary and human (stress) costs, and also for political expediency, some large corporations have entered a "steady state" with respect to their highly skilled workforce, and are seeking to curb further increases in their mobility by decentralising decision making and by engaging in more localised recruitment and use of their highly skilled staffs.

The application of new information technologies
The application of new information technologies will also tend to reduce the international migration of the highly skilled. Unlike the attributes of low-skilled migrant labour, which demand a physical presence in the performance of tasks, the main contribution of the highly skilled is knowledge. Knowledge can be transferred geographically in a number of ways not necessarily requiring a physical presence.

Modern satellite and fibre-optic communications, faxes and e-mail mean that specialists can be in almost instant touch with each other. Teleconferencing can already deal with routine business. The disadvantage of not being in the same room as the person with whom one is conferring is declining all the time, although the ultimate advantage of physical contact will never disappear in those sectors which traditionally place a premium on the quality of people and personality (O'Brien, 1992). However, new information technology enables a multiplication of possible meeting places, depending on the particular circumstances of the moment: to the modern PMT worker, office support and files are only a fax or modem away. It would be surprising if these facilities did not make some inroads into at least the growth of mobility among the highly skilled.

The intra-company transfer system is now under challenge. A growing problem, not yet captured in the statistics, is the use by foreign-owned companies of corporate transferees on what is effectively a labour sub-contract basis. The process has recently come under public scrutiny in the US, and is also appearing in the UK and elsewhere. In the UK it seems to occur particularly in computing/systems and banking. It especially affects Third World-based companies which are bringing in foreign staff on secondment to install hard- and software systems often at low salaries. Because these firm pay generally lower wages than those in the highly developed economies, they are often able to undercut Western companies when tendering for contracts. A further complication is that installation work can, increasingly, be done via satellite links, with only brief visits for checking purposes.

This process of bringing in what are in effect sub-contract staff calls into question current arrangements for the international migration of the highly skilled. In effect, the corporate transfer system is being used by foreign companies to bring in staff to compete with indigenous labour and UK companies. The practice seems likely to grow unless host countries take steps to curb it, including a review of their policies towards corporate transfer. Rising education levels and populations in less developed countries will inevitably lead to larger bodies of high level skills there, with rates of remuneration that will make them increasingly competitive in the provision of expertise – something that hitherto the developed economies could regard as their particular preserve.

Conclusions — where are we?

In recent years three major pressures upon western Europe have driven the policy debate: increased flows from the poor countries of the South; from the East; and a steep rise in asylum seeking. Labour market needs have scarcely been discussed.

The consequences of the ensuing search for solutions have spilled over into eastern Europe, where similar responses are being developed. The result has been to create a set of conditions in Europe within which policy concentration and harmonisation seems inexorable. The countries of central and eastern Europe want their borders to the West, particularly with the EU, to be as open as possible. The price of this is to control more stringently their eastern and southern borders. In this sense they are acting as western Europe's migration "frontier". As a result there is a concertation of border policies with regard to migration with both western and eastern Europe, and between them, leading towards a more harmonised approach in the continent as a whole.

It has become clear that mass migrations within and from eastern Europe and the former Soviet Union are unlikely. It is equally clear that large scale movements of population within and from eastern Europe will occur because they are freer societies. Tighter border controls in the region are inevitable, as the continent moves towards a pan-European pattern, but in the absence of an unwillingness to find and deport those without the necessary documentation, border controls by themselves will not reduce migration flows.

Almost no one advocates completely open borders for all. The main focus of debate now is the issue of orderly migration. Migrations do and will occur and recur; democracies, mindful of human rights and international obligations, are still learning how to manage them. Policies aiming at encouraging potential migrants to stay-at-home, through targeted aid and investment programmes for example, can only work in the long-term (OECD, 1994). They need to be balanced by measures designed to ensure that the migrations that do happen take place in an orderly and managed fashion. Most states have already established a set of priorities to be applied to potential migrants. Too often this has been done in ignorance of the true costs and benefits of various actions. The migration balance sheet is only beginning to be drawn up.

ANNEXE 5.1: FOREIGN POPULATION IN EEA COUNTRIES IN THOUSANDS (1 JANUARY 1993)

	AUS	BELG	DENM	FINL	FRA	GER	GRE	IREL	ITALY	LUX.	NETHS.	PORT	SPAIN	SWED	UK	ICELAND	LIEC	NORW	SWZ	EEA	EEA+Swz	EU TOT
EU (15)	79.4	541.6	40.5	12.3	1321.5	1719.2	64.7	55.5	160.3	115.9	189.0	32.7	181.8	187.0	768.0	2.4	5.0	57.7	826.6	6361.1		5469.4
EEA (18) + SWITZ	85.1	544.9	55.0	13.2	1345.7	1761.3	67.4	55.5	179.6	116.7	192.7	33.8	189.8	229.5	782.7	2.7	9.7	60.7	829.8	6555.8		5652.9
C & E EUROPE	64.4	7.2	8.0	17.4	63.0	716.2	29.4	0.0	63.6	0.0	11.9	0.8	6.3	30.1	45.6	0.4	0.0	4.8	22.4	1091.5		1063.9
OTHER EUROPE	317.5	95.7	45.0	1.3	250.2	2886.5	10.0	0.0	83.1	3.3	231.3	0.2	66.4	66.4	72.7	0.2	0.9	12.5	284.6	4427.8		4129.6
AFRICA	8.5	190.2	9.5	3.9	1633.1	283.9	19.6	0.0	284.4	1.3	203.3	52.0	71.3	25.4	203.7	0.1	0.0	11.3	23.9	3025.4		2990.1
AMERICA	9.5	20.2	8.2	2.7	72.8	168.8	29.2	8.9	148.7	1.6	49.6	29.4	89.3	38.2	280.0	0.8	0.2	18.0	33.0	1009.1		957.1
ASIA	25.7	25.3	43.3	5.8	227.0	594.7	39.1	0.0	158.0	1.2	61.4	4.8	33.6	88.9	544.7	0.5	0.9	45.1	47.8	1947.0		1853.5
AUSTRALIA & OCEANIA	0.7	0.6	0.9	0.4	2.3	8.4	0.0	0.0	5.1	0.0	3.0	0.4	0.7	1.7	76.2	0.1	0.0	0.7	1.9	105.3		102.6
STATELESS & UNKNOWN	6.2	25.1	10.2	1.6	2.5	76.0	3.4	25.5	1.0	4.6	4.0	0.2	0.9	15.6	14.0	0.0	0.6	0.8	-	192.2		190.8
TOTAL	517.6	909.2	180.1	46.3	3596.6	6495.8	200.3	89.9	923.5	128.7	757.2	121.6	458.3	495.8	2019.6	4.8	11.5	153.9	1243.4	18354.1		16940.5
% COLUMNS¹	AUS	BELG	DEN	FINL	FRA	GERM	GRE	IRL	ITALY	LUX	NETHS	PORT	SPAIN	SWED	UK	ICEL	LIECH	NOR	SWITZ	EEA	EEA+Swz	EU TOT
EU (15)	15.3	59.6	22.5	26.6	36.7	26.5	32.3	61.7	17.4	90.1	25.0	26.9	39.7	37.7	38.0	50.0	43.5	37.5	66.5	34.7		32.3
EEA (18) + SWITZ	16.4	59.9	30.5	28.5	37.4	27.1	33.6	61.7	19.4	90.7	25.4	27.8	41.4	46.3	38.8	56.3	84.3	39.4	66.7	35.7		33.4
C & E EUROPE	12.4	0.8	4.4	37.6	1.8	11.0	14.7	0.0	6.9	0.0	1.6	0.7	1.4	6.1	2.3	8.3	0.0	3.1	1.8	5.9		6.3
OTHER EUROPE	61.3	10.5	25.0	2.8	7.0	44.4	5.0	0.0	9.0	2.6	30.5	0.2	14.5	13.4	3.6	4.2	7.8	8.1	22.9	24.1		24.4
AFRICA	1.6	20.9	5.3	8.4	45.4	4.4	9.8	0.0	30.8	1.0	26.8	42.8	15.6	5.1	10.1	2.1	0.0	7.3	1.9	16.5		17.7
AMERICA	1.8	2.2	4.6	5.8	2.0	2.6	14.6	9.9	16.1	1.2	6.6	24.2	19.5	7.7	13.9	16.7	1.7	11.7	2.7	5.5		5.6
ASIA	5.0	2.8	24.0	12.5	6.3	9.2	19.5	0.0	17.1	0.9	8.1	3.9	7.3	17.9	27.0	10.4	0.9	29.3	3.8	10.6		10.9
AUSTRALIA & OCEANIA	0.1	0.0	0.5	0.9	0.1	0.1	1.1	0.0	0.6	0.0	0.4	0.3	0.2	0.3	3.8	2.1	0.0	0.5	0.2	0.6		0.6
STATELESS & UNKNOWN	1.2	2.8	5.7	3.5	0.1	1.2	1.7	28.4	0.1	3.6	0.5	0.2	0.2	3.1	0.7	0.0	5.2	0.5	-	1.0		1.1

% ROWS+	AUS	BELG	DEN	FINL	FRA	GERM	GRE	IRL	ITALY	LUX	NETHS	PORT	SPAIN	SWED	UK	ICEL	LIECH	NOR	SWITZ	EU TOT
EU (15)	1.2	8.5	0.6	0.2	20.8	27.0	1.0	0.9	2.5	1.8	3.0	0.5	2.9	2.9	12.1	0.0	0.0	0.9	13.0	84.73
EEA (18) + SWITZ	1.3	8.3	0.8	0.2	20.5	26.9	1.0	0.8	2.7	1.8	2.9	0.5	2.9	3.5	11.9	0.0	0.1	0.9	12.7	84.93
C & E.EUROPE	5.9	0.7	0.7	1.6	5.8	65.6	2.7	0.0	5.8	0.0	1.1	0.0	0.6	2.8	4.2	0.0	0.0	0.4	2.1	91.57
OTHER EUROPE	7.2	2.2	1.0	0.0	5.7	65.2	0.2	0.0	1.9	0.0	5.2	0.0	1.5	1.5	1.6	0.0	0.0	0.3	6.4	86.09
AFRICA	0.3	6.3	0.3	0.1	54.0	9.4	0.6	0.0	9.4	0.0	6.7	1.7	2.4	0.8	6.7	0.0	0.0	0.4	0.8	98.55
AMERICA	0.9	2.0	0.8	0.3	7.2	16.7	2.9	0.9	14.7	0.2	4.9	2.9	8.8	3.8	27.7	0.0	0.0	1.8	3.3	93.91
ASIA	1.3	1.3	2.2	0.3	11.7	30.5	2.0	0.0	8.1	0.0	3.2	0.2	1.7	4.6	28.0	0.0	0.0	2.3	2.5	93.88
AUSTRALIA & OCEANIA	0.7	0.6	0.9	0.4	2.2	8.0	2.1	0.0	4.8	0.0	2.8	0.4	0.7	1.6	72.4	0.0	0.0	0.7	1.8	96.77
STATELESS & UNKNOWN	3.2	13.1	5.3	0.8	1.3	39.5	1.8	13.3	0.5	2.4	2.1	0.1	0.5	8.1	7.3	0.0	0.3	0.4	-	96.05

Note: Stateless/Unknown excluded.
* Columns add up to 100%
+ the sum of the EEA and Switzerland is 100%
Source: Eurostat (1995)

ANNEXE 5.2: NET POPULATION FLOWS OF SELECTED WESTERN EUROPEAN COUNTRIES, 1980-1994 (THOUSANDS)

	1980	1981	1982	1983	1984	1985	1986	1987	1988	1989	1990	1991	1992	1993	1994*	Net TOT.
BELGIUM	13.4	5.2	0.8	3.0	8.0	9.9	11.6	11.3	13.6	20.7	30.2	33.7	33.1	31.2	33.3	259.0
DENMARK	0.4	-1.8	-0.1	1.7	4.0	6.2	11.0	6.2	0.5	8.3	8.3	10.9	11.5	11.1		76.6
FINLAND	-1.2	5.7	7.3	6.8	4.2	2.7	1.7	0.7	1.3	3.4	7.1	12.1	8.5	8.4	3.8	72.9
GERMANY	312.0	152.3	-75.4	-117.1	-151.1	83.4	215.8	481.9	977.2	1041.0	600.7	592.9	276.6	152.5		4731.1
ICELAND	-0.5	0.2	0.6	0.2	-0.3	-0.5	-0.3	1.2	1.5	-1.1	-0.7	1.0	-0.3	-0.2		0.8
IRELAND**								-23.0	-41.9	-43.9	-23.0	-2.0	2.0	-6.0	-10.0	-147.8
ITALY		44.1	1.2	25.8	24.1	62.2	59.6	91.7	74.2	43.8	138.1	69.2				634.0
LUXEMBOURG+	1.4	0.4	-0.3	0.0	0.5	0.8	1.9	2.4	3.1	2.9	3.9	4.2	4.3	4.2	4.0	33.7
N'LANDS	53.0	17.0	3.2	6.0	8.0	24.1	32.7	43.9	35.4	39.2	60.0	62.9	58.1	59.7	37.2	540.4
NORWAY	4.1	5.2	5.7	4.3	3.8	6.2	7.5	13.8	10.1	-1.5	1.7	8.0	9.9	11.8	7.4	98.0
SPAIN											21.9	15.2				37.1
SWEDEN	9.6	2.8	2.0	2.2	8.7	11.1	15.0	22.0	29.6	44.4	34.9	25.0	19.6	12.1		239.0
SWITZERLAND++	6.8	16.3	12.1	-3.4	3.0	5.1	14.0	17.7	20.3	22.9	41.8	43.4	31.7	32.8	275.0	539.5
UK§	-55.4	-79.5	-57.2	17.0	37.2	58.6	36.9	2.1	-21.2	44.4	36.0	27.6	-11.1	-3.0	60.0	92.4
																7206.7

Sources: Eurostat, OECD and national statistics.
* 1994 data from National Statistical Offices etc. in the 1995 reports to the OECD by the individual country SOPEMI Correspondents.
** 1992-1994 estimated flows.
+ 1980-94 data from STATEC in the 1995 report to the OECD by the Luxembourg SOPEMI Correspondent.
++ 1994 figure rounded.
§ 1993-1994 figures rounded to the nearest '000.

Endnotes

1. This chapter is derived from a longer analysis prepared by the author for the Council of Europe: Current Trends in International Migration in Europe, Strasbourg, 1995. The assistance of James Clarke in preparing this chapter is gratefully acknowledged.
2. Those for Germany, for example, exclude ethnic Germans. Unfortunately reliable data on outflows of workers are not available, making it impossible to produce net labour flows.

References

Coleman DA (1992) "Does Europe need immigrants? Population and workforce projections", *International Migration Review*, 26, pp413–61.

Eurostat (1995) *Migration Statistics*, Luxembourg.

International Centre For Migration Policy Development (ICMPD) (1994) *The key to Europe – a comparative analysis of entry and asylum policies in Western countries*, Swedish Government Official Reports 1994:135. Ministry of Culture. Stockholm: Norstedts Tryckeri AB.

O'Brien P (1992) "German-Polish migration: the elusive search for a German nation-state", *International Migration Review*, 26, pp373–87.

OECD (1994) *Migration and Development: New Partnerships for Co-operation*, OECD, Paris.

OECD (1995) *Trends in International Migration*, OECD, Paris.

Russell SS, and Teitelbaum MS (1992) *International migration and international trade*, World Bank discussion papers, 160. 1st Ed. Washington DC: International Bank for Reconstruction and Development/The World Bank.

Salt J, Mervin J & Shortland J (1993) "The Cost of International Relocation", *Relocation News*, 26, pp4–7.

Salt J, Singleton A & Hogarth J (1994) *Europe's International Migrants*, HMSO, London.

Werner H (1995) *Economic Integration and Migration: the European Case*, Labour Market Research Topics series, no. 12, Nürnberg, Institut für Arbeitsmarkt- und Berufsforschung.

Widgren J (1994) *Multilateral Co-operation to Combat Trafficking in Migrants and the Role of International Organizations*, Eleventh IOM Seminar on Migration 26-28 October 1994, Geneva: International Response to Trafficking in Migrants and the Safeguarding of Migrant Rights, Paper Number 6. Geneva: International Organization for Migration (IOM).

6. Old and new labour migration to Germany from Eastern Europe[1]

Elmar Hönekopp

Introduction

Since the end of World War II Germany has received millions of newcomers, including displaced Germans, immigrants, and migrant workers. These newcomers came from all parts of Europe and from various areas of the world, and included persons of a variety of ethnic origins and nationalities.

Since 1989, Germany has once again become a major recipient of immigrants. Between 1989 and 1992, the net movement of people into Germany was an average of over one million persons annually, mostly into the former West Germany, and mostly for economic reasons. Immigration is still going on, although at a lower level.

This paper firstly summarises post-war migration to Germany in order to put migration patterns since 1989 in context. Secondly, we outline the current migration patterns and the employment of foreigners, concentrating on the various programs through which migrant workers are arriving in Germany. Thirdly, the implications of using worker programs as a substitute for both illegal immigration and a comprehensive immigration policy are explored for Germany and for the countries that the migrants come from.

Migration to Germany after World War II

Germany has been affected by migration since the end of World War II. However, the migrant influx is much steadier than the politics surrounding migration. There were six major migration waves (for details see Hönekopp, 1994).

The first, from 1945 to 1950, brought eight million refugees and displaced persons from the former German eastern regions to West Germany.

In the second phase, from 1950 to 1961, (the year the Berlin Wall was built), about four million *Übersiedler* from East Germany moved to West Germany, plus additional *Aussiedler* from the ex-Soviet Union. Since 1950, some 3.3 million *Aussiedler* have moved to Germany.[2]

These first two migration waves consisted mostly of Germans. The third wave, which began in the late 1950s and lasted until 1973, brought millions of foreign or guest workers to Germany. Under recruitment agreements with their countries of origin, workers from Italy, Greece, Yugoslavia, Turkey, Spain, Portugal, Morocco, and Tunisia arrived in Germany to fill vacant jobs for temporary periods of one to three years. Between 1960 and 1973, some 18.5 million foreigners arrived in Germany, and 4.7 million settled. Recruitment was halted during the oil crisis of 1973.

The recruitment ban marked the beginning of the fourth wave, when many guest workers who had settled in Germany unified their families there, signalling their intention to remain in Germany. The recruitment ban undoubtedly encouraged the settlement of guest workers in Germany.

The fifth wave began in the 1980s, and is marked by the arrival of ethnic German *Aussiedler,* mostly from Poland, the Soviet Union and Romania, and an increasing number of applicants for asylum, who came from Turkey and from Eastern European countries such as Poland and Romania.

The current sixth wave, which began in 1988, is characterised, firstly, by *Aussiedler* from Eastern Europe and *Übersiedler* – now internal migrants – from the GDR; secondly by quite large numbers of foreign nationals who come from the same countries as the *Aussiedler* (above all from Poland, but also now from the former Soviet Union) and thirdly by asylum seekers, whose numbers peaked in 1992, although there continue to be large numbers of applicants from Africa and Asia and former Yugoslavia.

This short survey shows that migration has been a continuous feature of the Federal Republic of Germany. However, the immigrants in this recent flow are not considered "foreigners", since *Übersiedler* and *Aussiedler* are, under the German *Grundgesetz* (constitution), German citizens; thus the government smoothed their entry by emphasising that these newly-arrived citizens had suffered in their countries of origin because they were Germans.

Current Migration Patterns

General migration since the eighties
Eastern Europeans began migrating to Germany before 1989. In Poland in the early 1980s, for example, the struggle for power between Solidarnosc and the Communist government led to Polish migration – of both ethnic Germans and non-German Poles – to Germany and other Western European and non-European countries. In 1981, for example, some 46,000 ethnic Germans and 93,000 non-German Poles arrived in Germany. Most were considered victims of oppression, although a few were project-tied workers, and Germany easily accepted them. Immigration from Poland increased in the second half of the 1980s.

During the 1980s, there was also a flow of Romanians to Germany. About two-thirds were ethnic Germans, for whom the German government paid the Romanian government 10,000 DM each, to repay Romania for its education and other human investments. (For a more detailed picture of the migration process to Germany see Chies and Hönekopp 1990, Hönekopp 1991, Faßmann and Münz 1994.)

The year 1989 marked a new era in east-west migration. First, more Poles migrated West, some to work, and others to sell goods in so-called Polish Markets. Second, East Germans began arriving in West Germany, first via Hungary and Czechoslovakia, and later directly. The number of ethnic Germans doubled between 1988 and 1989, while the number of asylum seekers from eastern Europe, Turkey and non-European countries increased.

In 1989, almost one million more people migrated into West Germany than emigrated, and net immigration remained at about 1 million annually through to 1992. This is a high rate of immigration given a population of 60 million (compare this to the USA, where net immigration is 600,000 with a population of 250 million, Germany has been the main destination for migrants from the East since the beginning of the new migration wave (see Hönekopp 1995).

Migration of foreigners
Between 1974 and 1994, Germany received a net total of 1.9 million foreign (non-German) migrants. Immigration from the East has increased so much in recent years, that half of the net 1.9 million are from eastern Europe and the former USSR. Indeed, more migrants left than entered Germany from the guest worker "recruitment" countries, including a net emigration of EU

Table 6.1: Net Immigration from eastern Europe* to Germany
1988–1994 (thousands)

	1988	1989	1990	1991	1992	1993	1994	1988-94
Net immigration (CEEC)	289	460	501	298	380	193	248	2,369
Germans (from CEEC)	155	297	348	193	212	211	194	1,610
Foreigners (from CEEC)	134	163	153	105	168	-18	54	759
(For comparison)								
Net immigration (Total)	442	597	688	601	788	472	330	3,918
Germans (Total)	153	265	312	178	195	195	177	1,475
Foreigners (Total)	289	332	376	423	593	277	153	2,443

* Bulgaria, former CSFR, Hungary, Poland, Romania, former USSR
Note: up to 1989 Western Germany, from 1990 onward: total Germany
Source: Federal Statistical Office of Germany; calculation by the author

nationals. This means that immigration, especially from Poland, more than compensated for emigration to Italy and former guest worker countries (net immigration from eastern Europe over the period was 850,000, including 500,000 Poles).

But between 1988 and 1994, some 5.8 million foreigners immigrated, and 3.4 million emigrated, producing net immigration of 2.4 million (see Table 6.1). Net immigration from the classic guest worker countries was about 1 million, due to migration of war refugees from the ex-Yugoslavia and asylum seekers from Turkey, but much of the net migration came from Eastern European countries (net 760,000) and Asian countries (net 262,000). In 1993, however, about 20,000 more east Europeans emigrated from than immigrated to Germany, although in 1994 there was again a net immigration of eastern Europeans to Germany, although on a lower level (see Fig. 6.1 and Table 6.1).

Former guest worker countries continue to send a significant number of immigrants to Germany. In 1974, immigration from the former countries in which guest workers were recruited constituted two thirds of immigration. It fell to one third in 1991, and rose to 40 per cent of net immigration in 1993, largely because of immigration from ex-Yugoslavia and Turkey. The eastern European share of net immigration rose from five per cent to nearly 40 per cent, with Poles alone making up about one quarter of all immigrants.

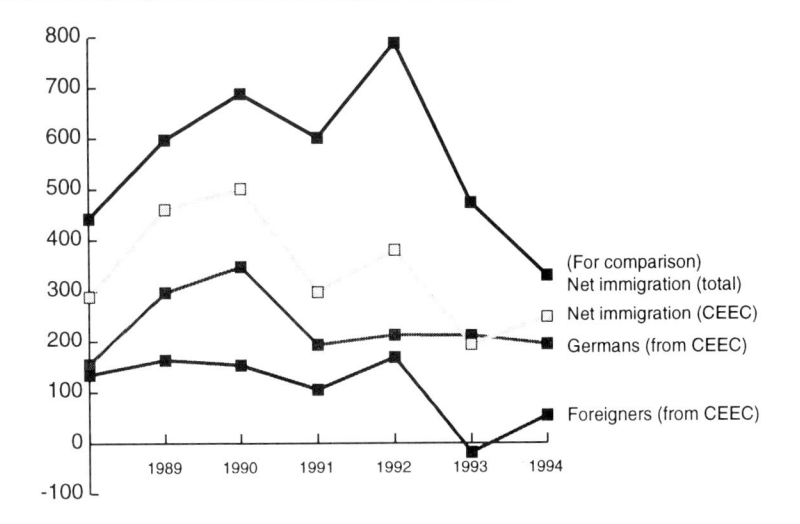

Fig. 6.1: Net immigration from Eastern Europe to Germany
1988–1994 (thousands)
Source: Federal Statistical Office

Migration of Germans
Since 1977, a net 100,000 Germans have emigrated to EC-countries, to America, Australia/Pacific countries, and to Austria, while a net 1.9 million Germans migrated to Germany from eastern Europe. For the years 1988–1994, net immigration of Germans from eastern Europe was higher than total net immigration (see Table 6.1). That means, that there was a small net out-migration of Germans to the other parts of the world.

Most German immigrants are today from eastern Europe, the figure being 80 per cent in 1993. And 94 per cent of east European migrants came from the ex-USSR. The trend of immigration from eastern Europe has now been stabilised, mostly because Germany has changed its regulations in terms of persons from the ex-USSR.

Migration today
Immigration to Germany today is still to a large extent a flow from the east. This immigration has the peculiarity that both ethnic Germans and other immigrants from eastern European have had and partly still have various advantages upon arrival. Most had been assumed to be political refugees, giving them confidence that they would not be returned, and permitting them immediate access to the labour market.

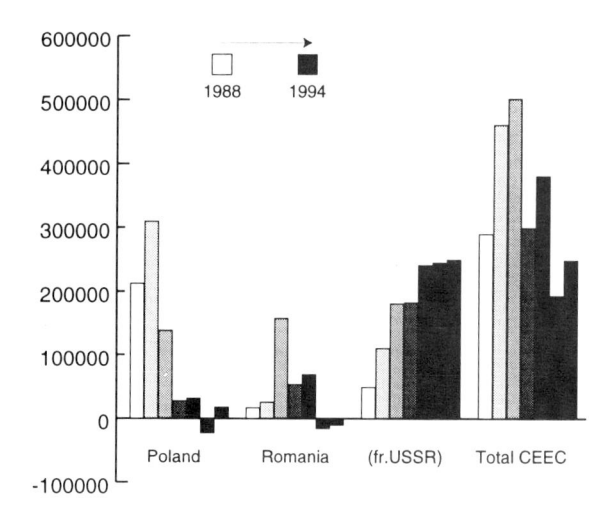

Figure 6.2: Balance of total migration from/to central and eastern European countries for Germany, 1988-1994
Source: Federal Statistical Office

About 90 per cent of the *Aussiedler* from eastern Europe are recognised as German citizens, and thus have immediate access to the German labour market, social benefits, and special integration benefits. It has proven difficult to integrate many *Aussiedler*, since their German language abilities and skill levels have been falling. However, Germany provides extensive language and vocational skills courses for *Aussiedler*.

The migration balance for the years after 1988 shows that east European migrants to Germany mainly came from three countries: Poland, Romania and the former Soviet Union (see Fig. 6.2 and Table 6.2). In recent years emigration to eastern Europe has increased alongside immigration, suggesting that many migrants are so-called birds of passage seeking to earn money in Germany; there is now a trend to net emigration (returns migration) to eastern Europe. Some established eastern Europeans have emigrated to take advantage of opportunities at home, including some Poles. In addition, five of six eastern European countries of origin have decreased rates of immigration to Germany. Only migration from the area of former Soviet Union is still clearly increasing, due to immigration of foreigners and ethnic Germans.

Table 6.2: Total inflows* from central & eastern European countries into Germany 1988-1994

Country	1988	1989	1990	1991	1992	1993	1994
Bulgaria	1,289	2,275	11,193	17,420	31,523	27,350	10,478
(fr.) CSFR	11,978	17,130	16,948	24,438	37,295	22,078	18,316
Hungary	12,966	15,372	16,708	25,676	28,652	24,853	19,803
Poland	313,792	455,075	300,693	145,663	143,709	81,740	88,132
Romania	20,233	29,483	174,388	84,165	121,291	86,559	34,567
(fr.) USSR	54,725	121,378	192,820	195,272	254,731	271,877	288,022
Total CEEC	414,983	640,713	712,750	492,634	617,201	514,457	459,318

* Foreigners and Germans
Source: Federal Statistical Office

This current development might strongly depend on the economic situation in Germany in 1993 and 1994. East Europeans could not find enough jobs and were to a less extent given permission to work. At the same time, the economic situation in some of the CEE countries has improved, so that migrants or potential migrants might have better chances to be economically active at home.

Immigration and population development

Population growth depends on natural increase – births minus deaths – and net immigration. The natural increase of the resident population in Germany is negative. However, net immigration caused the German population to increase by an average of more than 500,000 per year since 1989, giving a population growth rate of about 0.6 per cent.

These overall demographic trends conceal the fact that the former East Germany is shrinking through both natural decrease and internal migration. Very few immigrants move to the former East Germany. In western Germany, by contrast, the population of 66 million, has experienced a net increase of about 1.5 per cent annually in recent years.

In 1995 foreigners made up about nine per cent of the total German population, and eleven per cent of the West German population, up from

Table 6.3: Total and Foreign Population by Selected Nationalities in Germany* 1989-1994

Nationality	1989	1990	1991	1992	1993	1994
Bulgaria	5,670	14,711	32,627	59,094	56,709	44,848
(fr.) CSFR	31,695	34,393	46,702	63,724	77,218	63,379
Hungary	31,627	36,733	56,401	61,436	62,195	57,986
Poland	220,443	242,013	271,198	285,553	260,514	263,381
Romania	21,101	60,293	92,135	167,327	162,577	125,861
(fr.) USSR	11,533	21,750	54,964	79,049	118,845	140,146
Total CEEC	322,069	409,893	554,027	716,183	738,058	695,601
Total For.	4,845,882	5,342,532	5,882,267	6,495,792	6,878,117	6,990,510
Total	62,063,000	79,565,000	79,884,000	80,595,000	81,190,000	81,410,000
CEEC/ Foreign Pop. (%)	6.6	7.7	9.4	11.0	10.7	10.0
CEEC/ Total Pop. (%)	0.5	0.5	0.7	0.9	0.9	0.9

* 1989: western Germany; from 1990 onwards total Germany
Source:Federal Statistical Office; calculations by the author

eight per cent in West Germany in 1989. Foreigners from the former guest worker countries still accounted for 62 per cent of all foreigners in 1995. The numerical significance of east Europeans foreigners is the German population is still very low, although in absolute tems their numbers have almost doubled (see Table 6.3). One should note that these data also include the immigration of non-German family members, coming with husbands or wives who are of ethnic German origin. On the other hand, eastern European immigrants of ethnic German origin are counted as Germans in the population register after their settlement.

The rapid increase in population due to immigration has created tensions in West Germany, as competition for housing, jobs, and education and other social services intensifies. The cost of unification prevented a rapid expansion of government services for immigrants. Indeed, the funds available for schooling and German language courses to help integrate ethnic German immigrants has been reduced. However, it is not easy to analyse the consequences of recent changes in integration efforts on the prospects for the *Aussiedler* because, once they are accepted as German citizens, there are no official statistics on them (except on their status as unemployed for a period of five years after their entrance to Germany). There is only limited information from special surveys.

Because of the various direct effects of immigration of *Aussiedler* on society (see above), a discussion has started again concerning further restriction of entrance to Germany.

Migration from the East and the labour market in Germany

General development

Most migrants from the east come to Germany for economic reasons, and the younger and best educated eastern Europeans have proven most keen to migrate. This migration affects labour markets in both eastern Europe and Germany.

In the Federal Republic of Germany the number of employees increased by 1.9 million (or nine per cent) between 1989 and 1992, and then fell by one million between 1992 and 1995. The number of foreigners employed has risen by 26 per cent since 1989, including a 285 per cent increase in the employment of east Europeans, from 54,000 in 1989 (see Table 6.4). But these

Table 6.4: Total, Foreign and east European Employees in western Germany *1989 – 1995** (thousands)

	1989	1990	1991	1992	1993	1994	1995
Total	21,619.3	22,368.1	23,173.4	23,530.3	23,122.5	22,755.3	22,597.3
Total foreign	1,689.3	1,782.3	1,898.5	2,036.2	2,183.6	2,140.5	2,128.7
East-Europeans[+]	54.6	72.2	100.3	143.0	170.4	157.6	157.6
East-Europeans as % of total employees	0.3	0.3	0.4	0.6	0.7	0.7	0.7
East-Europeans as % of total foreign emp.	3.2	4.1	5.3	7.0	7.8	7.4	7.4

*   western Germany only (employment of foreigners in eastern Germany is not significant)
** at June of each year
\+   Bulgaria, (fr.) CSFR, Hungary, Poland, Romania, (fr.) USSR
Source: Federal Employment Services – Statistics on members of the compulsory social insurance system

data understate east European employment, mainly because they do not show the contribution of immigrant ethnic Germans from eastern Europe. In addition, the data reflect employment on 30 June of each year, when many seasonal workers are not yet employed; they include only socially insured workers, which means they exclude project-tied workers who are not socially insured in Germany; and they partly include seasonal workers, since compulsory social insurance only applies with a working period of more than 50 days, which means that a lot of employers try to employ seasonal workers for no longer than those 50 days so as to avoid additional labour costs. The actual number of eastern Europeans employed in Germany may be 50 per cent higher than the official count of 160,000 in 1994.

Using the official data one finds that Eastern European workers as a percentage of total employees increased from 0.3 per cent in 1989 to only 0.7 per cent in 1995. East Europeans as percentage of total foreign employees count now for about seven per cent. On these figures, it appears that legal employment of foreigners from eastern Europe in Germany is not very important.

Special employment opportunities for Eastern Europeans in Germany
From 1988 onwards, even before the fall of the iron curtain, large numbers of Poles came to neighbouring Germany, trying to find employment opportunities. After 1989, this movement increased and needed to be controlled, because it was feared it would endanger wages and social standards.

Within the negotiations on German unification, during 1990 the Polish government was offered special work opportunities for workers intending to go abroad. In fact, the Federal Republic of Germany made such agreements with almost all eastern European countries in 1990 and 1991, that permit east European workers to find at least temporary employment in Germany. This is very unique in Europe, although there are small programs or employment opportunities for eastern Europeans in some other European countries (see Werner 1995). There are five distinct programs (see Table 6.5).

Table 6.5: East European Program Workers in Germany 1991-1995

Program	1991	1992	1993	1994	1995
Project tied workers*	51,770	93,592	67,270	39,070	47,565
Seasonal workers** +	90,000	212,000	164,377	140,656	176,590
Border commuters*	7,000	12,400	11,200	8,000	8,500
"New Guest workers"**	2,234	5,057	5,771	5,529	5,478
Nurses**	-	1,455	506	412	367
Total	151,004	324,504	249,124	193,667	238,500

Note: including program workers from former Yugoslavia
* persons employed; yearly average on monthly basis
** job placements
+ annual employment volume equivalent might be a fourth to a fifth of the mentioned figures
Source: Central Placement Unit and Headquarters of Federal Employment Services. Border commuters: calculated by the author (1995: estimation)

- *Project-tied work.* This permits a German firm to subcontract part of a project to a foreign firm, which then supplies the workers to fulfil the subcontract. The workers' stay in Germany is tied to the project contract between the German and foreign firm. A certain maximum number is permitted per year, which varies year by year, and with quotas for various countries. In 1992, 100,000 foreign workers were allowed into Germany on project-tied contracts. In 1993 and 1994 the total quota was reduced to about 50,000, in reaction to complaints from German firms of unfair competition, although it is now slightly increasing again. Some special regional labour market criteria have been introduced concerning the granting of work permits for project-tied workers. The contracting companies are obliged to make sure that subcontracter companies pay their workers the standard wage for that branch. Project-tied workers are not covered by social security contributions in Germany, but have to be insured in their home country. That means that labour costs for those workers are much less than for resident workers even if everything is done legally. In fact, project-tied workers are often paid much lower wages than the standard, and are not socially insured. Project-tied work takes place mainly in construction or in related activities.

- *Seasonal work.* This permits foreign workers to work in Germany for up to three months per year (showmen and fair workers up to nine months) if workers are not available in Germany to fill vacant jobs. In order to employ seasonal foreign workers, a German employer requests them, usually by name, and then the foreigners are issued 90-day work permits. Since late 1993, the employment of eastern Europeans within this program has been restricted mainly to farming and the processing of farm products, to hotels and restaurants and to showman and fair worker activities, since employers liked to use them for regular jobs (very often, eg in construction, to fill gaps during vacation season). Officially, they have to be paid the usual wage. But "usual" wages are quite low in these areas. Seasonal workers are mainly employed in agriculture and related activities (1993: 62 per cent, 1994: 92 per cent) and in hotels and restaurants (about four per cent). The largest part are from Poland (1993: 79 per cent, 1994 and 1995: 88 per cent). The numbers of employed persons within this program is high. But it has to be realised that these figures are only for placements. Since the working stay is limited to three months maximum, the actual yearly employment volume is much less (see the re-calculation in the next section).

- *Border commuters.* These are Polish and Czech residents living within 50 km of the German border who can work in Germany, if German employers can convince local labour offices that local workers are not available. Border commuters must still reside in their country of origin and return daily to them. Alternatively they can work in Germany for a maximum of two days a week before returning to their respective countries. Marginal part-time work is not permitted. Work contracts are obligatory, including payment of official wages. The total numbers employed are quite small (1995: about 6,500 Czech and 2,000 Polish commuters).

- *Guest workers.* These are agreements for exchange programs that permit young East Europeans and Germans to go to another country to enlarge their occupational skills or knowledge of language through work stays. They earn regular wages. Participants must be 18 to 40, have completed vocational education, and have a basic knowledge of the language of the destination country. But there are no definite entrance criteria concerning special training measures during the work stay. They can remain abroad for up to 18 months. The number of participants is restricted, eg a maximum 1,400 from the Czech Republic and the Slovakian Republic, 1,000 from Poland, and 2,000 from Hungary, for a total of 10,000. Up to now, almost no German workers have gone to neighbouring countries. Altogether, the number of employed persons within this program is quite low. Only half of the allowed maximum is used. 80 per cent of the actual employment is from Poland, the Czech and Slovak republics and from Hungary.

- *Foreign nurses.* There were about 400 placements (only from the former Yugoslavia) in 1994 and a bit less in 1995.

These programmes provide opportunities for east Europeans to work legally in Germany. The purpose of these programs is:

- to provide jobs for eastern Europeans and assist the east European countries to alleviate their labour market situation and to provide income transfers that can help economic development

- to give eastern European workers a chance to improve their knowledge of western working and production standards through on the job experience or special training schemes

- to find workers for special labour demand in Germany

- to convert illegal into legal workers

- to avoid permanent immigration by definite restrictions on work stay and so to maintain the manageability of the additional workforce

All five goals have been fulfilled but only to a certain extent. For example, concerning goal one: the alleviation of the home countries' labour market problems is not as high as it seems at a first glance. The real employment figures are much less than the high placement figures. Meanwhile, it is sometimes the case that the removal of workers from certain areas or sectors to Germany induces some pressure on regional or occupational labour markets in their home countries. However, income transfers from Eastern European workers to their home countries do seem to be important, especially for Poland.

The goal of knowledge improvement can also work only partially. A larger part of the east Europeans in Germany, above all project-tied and seasonal workers, will not be able to learn very much because of their special work situation, although the new guest worker program aims to provide participants with skills useful for accelerating the development of the economies of their own countries. However since there is no real training obligation for the employer and for the worker as an entrance criteria to that program, this scheme is often used as a means of cheaper labour. And workers with skills very often seem more willing to work at jobs that pay relatively high wages for a limited period of time, rather than take jobs that offer training wages, eg skilled Poles may prefer harvesting grapes or apples to extending their knowledge of machine operation in a factory.

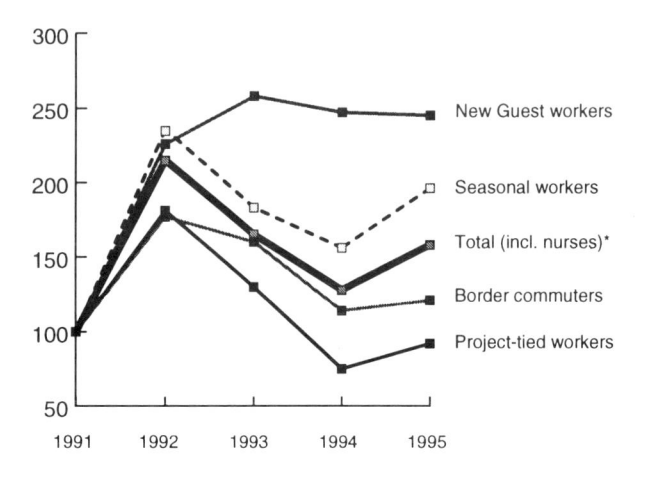

Fig. 6.3: East European program workers in Germany, 1991–1995
(Indices, 1991=100)
Source: Federal Employment Services

The goal of finding workers to satify labour demand in Germany may have been fulfilled. East European program workers are concentrated in low-level jobs, partly because there are relatively few jobs available for skilled east Europeans in Germany and because low paid jobs (in agriculture) and jobs with poor working conditions are not accepted by resident workers (like in hotels and restaurants).

It is difficult to estimate to what extent the goal of converting illegal into legal work has succeded. The question is what would have happened without these work programmes. In the field of seasonal agricultural work the attempt to legalise work appears very successful; in the field of construction only partially. There are some abuses within each of the programs, such as an employer of seasonal workers illegally lending them to another employer, or the workers staying longer than three months. There are also complaints that the foreign workers depress wages, especially in construction. But the major problem is that there are still a significant number of illegal workers, perhaps as many illegal workers as legal workers. And the work programs (seasonal work and above all project-tied work) are partly used as doors to illegal work. Investigation measures have been intensified, but it is difficult to maintain control.

Table 6.6: Yearly Employment Equivalents for east European Program Workers in Germany 1991–1995

Program	1991	1992	1993	1994	1995
Project tied workers*	51,770	93,592	67,270	39,070	47,565
Seasonal workers**	18,375	43,283	35,341	28,717	36,054
Border commuters+	7,000	12,400	11,200	8,000	8,500
"New Guest workers"++	1,500	4,000	5,200	5,400	5,400
Nurses§	-	1,000	1,800	2,100	2,200
Total	**78,645**	**154,275**	**120,811**	**83,287**	**99,719**

Note: including program workers from former Yougoslavia
* persons employed; yearly average on monthly basis
** adapted figures, see text
+ yearly average on quarterly basis
++ estimated yearly equivalants
§ persons employed, estimated cumulative figures
Source: Estimated by the author

The goal of avoiding permanent migration is a very important one. From the beginning of enlarged immigration from eastern Europe, the German government tried to restrict the work stay to a very short duration, without any rights for permanent stay in any case. This goal has so far been achieved, at least as far legal employment is concerned. So it remained possible to alter the additional workforce from the East in response to the economic demand for labour, as shown by the changes in the program worker figures (see Fig. 6.3): after 1992, it was possible to reduce the number of workers in the main programs substantially in the face of lower demand.

Actual employment of East European workers in Germany
Official figures (Table 6.5) show that there was a sharp increase in employment of eastern European workers in Germany after 1989. But these data understate east European employment, for reasons discussed earlier.

At the same time the importance of the employment of east Germans, especially of seasonal workers, is overestimated by only having a look at the placement figures. Since the duration of work per year is only up to three months, the figures have to be re-calculated to get a measure of yearly employment equivalents. The results of this re-calculation are given above in Table 6.6. The spectacular placement figures for seasonal workers are very

Table 6.7: Total, foreign and east-European employees in western Germany on adapted figures 1990 – 1995 (Yearly Averages, thousands)

	1990	1991	1992	1993	1994	1995
Total employees	22,396	23,349	23,639	23,200	22,855	22,662
Germans	20,586	21,383	21,469	20,948	20,667	20,469
Foreigners	1,820	1,966	2,170	2,252	2,188	2,193
East-European employees	109	165	256	243	208	222
East-Europeans as % of total employees (%)	0.5	0.7	1.1	1.0	0.9	1.0
East-Europeans as % of total foreign employees (%)	6.0	8.4	11.8	10.8	9.5	10.1

Note: Original figures as in Table 6.4, adapted as explained in the text

modest in terms of yearly employment volumes (1992: 43,000, 1995: 36,000, compared with 212,000 and 177,000).

The figures for "New Guest Workers" and for nurses also have to be adapted to yearly volumes. Here, however, only rough estimations are possible. A full picture of yearly employment equivalents for east European program workers is given in Table 6.6 (previous page).

To get the real numbers of foreign East European employment in Germany, seasonal workers not registered for social insurance and project-tied workers have to be added to the official data. The others are registered in the compulsory social insurance scheme.

This re-calculation (see Table 6.7 above) shows the importance of foreign East European employment to be slightly higher than shown by official data (compare Table 6.4). But despite of all that, the share in total employment remains modest (one per cent), with a share in foreign employment of tenper cent.

In summary we see that during the first half of the nineties there was a remarkable rise in the employment of eastern European workers compared to a much slower increase of employment of all foreigners and almost no growth of total employment (see Fig. 6.4). Program workers contributed to

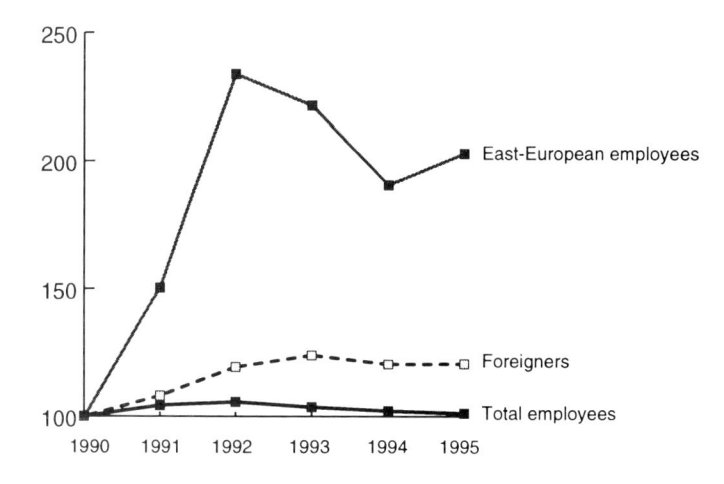

Fig. 6.4: Total, foreign and east European employees in west Germany, 1990-1995
Adapted figures, indices

this development by only about half of the total increase of east European employment. Others are either persons with a longer duration of stay and /or family members of immigrated ethnic Germans.

Employment of east European workers: importance for the labour market in Germany
The new wave of immigration and inflow which started at the end of a decade was characterised by very intensive restructuring of the labour market and by resulting contradictory developments of employment and unemployment (see Figs. 6.5 and 6.6). In the first half of the decade there was a stagnation of total employment and a clear decrease of employment of foreigners, accompanied by a sharp rise of unemployment (doubling of total and tripling of foreign unemployment). In the second half of the decade these tendencies turned with an increase of employment (total and especially foreign), and, with a delayed reaction, of decreasing unemployment (however, remaining far above the level at the beginning of the decade).

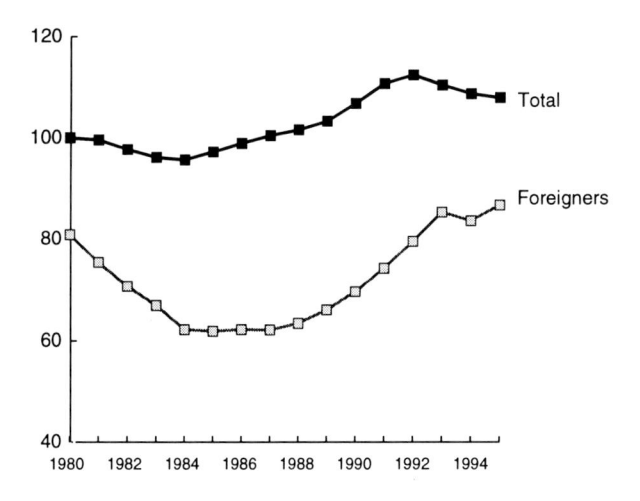

Fig. 6.5: Employment (total and foreigners) in West Germany, 1980–1994

index; 1973=100

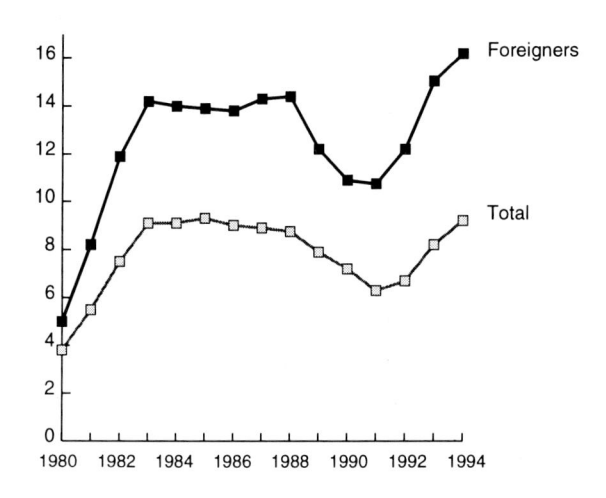

Fig. 6.6: Unemployment Rates (total and Foreigners), yearly average 1980–1994

Source (both graphs): Federal Employment Services

At the end of the decade, these positive trends had been reinforced by the economic effects of the unification of both Germanys on the demand for goods and on the resulting demand for additional labour. At that point, the new immigrants had flown into the labour market, available at the right time. Because of the macro-economic situation the German economy was able to absorb both immigrant and temporary workers until 1992. In this situation, immigration had a positive effect on the economy and on jobs (see Gieseck *et al*, 1994).

But in late 1992, there were clear signs that the positive economic effects of the German unification process had come to an end, with decreasing demand for goods, decreasing employment and again a sharp increase of unemployment, above all for foreigners. This situation has been intensified by the integration of the East European economies into the international economy. The import of cheaper goods endangers especially – but not only – low paid jobs in certain branches in Germany, and the available cheap and qualified labour in neighbouring eastern countries results in German investments in this area, again negatively effecting employment in certain German industries, reducing jobs for Germans and foreigners in Germany.

The steadily rising unemployment since 1992 made it harder for East European workers to find jobs in Germany. This is one general reason why the number of opportunities for East Europeans to work in Germany has been reduced. The number of program workers has been cut down since 1992 by a quarter, the number of foreign employees from Eastern Europe by a fifth (see Tables 6.5 and 6.7). Since the share of program workers makes up only about a half of total East European employment, the question has to be raised; is a further reduction, firstly, technically and politically possible and, secondly, economically adequate and convenient?

The answer to the first part of the question is, of course, two-fold: a further reduction is technically possible, and the implemented program regulations allow a very quick adaptation to current demand; but the other point is the political dimension. Having in mind the historical background and the genesis of the programmes, the conclusion must be that further reductions would involve friction with the contracting countries. In addition, the ability to achieve the main goals as described above would disappear, especially the goal of providing workers for special labour demand and the goal of converting illegal into legal work.

As far as the second part of the question is concerned, the answer may partly be provided by looking at the current discussion in Germany about employment of east Europeans. There are two main arguments: first, that there is labour demand for jobs for which no resident workers are available and, second, that there is too much pressure from labour supply in one sector: construction.

Regarding the first, the argument is conducted almost exclusively between employers (farmers etc.), seeking enough workers from eastern Europe, and labour administrations, trying to place residents in work (the long-term unemployed, asylum seekers, unqualified persons). Every year is like a game: employers name a certain amount of demand, which is reduced to a certain extent by the labour administration, offering some resident unemployed. There is today no general public interest in this discussion.

The second argument is more meaningful. After German unification, construction was one of the main beneficiaries of the additional demand for goods and services. But it is now under pressure from three directions: First, the general demand for construction products has been reduced. Secondly, within the European Union the construction industry is now much more competitive than before because of the so-called freedom of services and settlement (allowing European construction companies, eg from Portugal or Spain, to work with their own and cheaper workers in Germany). Thirdly, the legal and illegal labour supply from various sources is strongly growing. The competition for jobs in the construction sector is between resident workers, legal and illegal workers from eastern Europe, the mainly illegal so-called pseudo-self-employed[3] and the low-paid legal workers of European construction companies.

Legal employment of east Europeans does not play a very important role in this discussion. One reason is that already by 1993 the admission criteria for project tied work had been tightened up and that – as shown – the numbers of project tied workers had been cut down. The other reason is that the main problem in this context are the illegal workers (pseudo-self-employed and illegals, also from eastern Europe) and the European workers working with their construction companies in Germany. The main concern of the current discussion is how to avoid low wages which resident workers are unable to compete with. A special law has been passed by the German parliament, trying to introduce minimum wages in construction and related branches, but it faces opposition from the German Employers Association (BDA).

Of what importance then, is the employment of east Europeans in sectors of the German economy and what effects could it have on the development of total employment and of unemployment? Since 1979 east Europeans

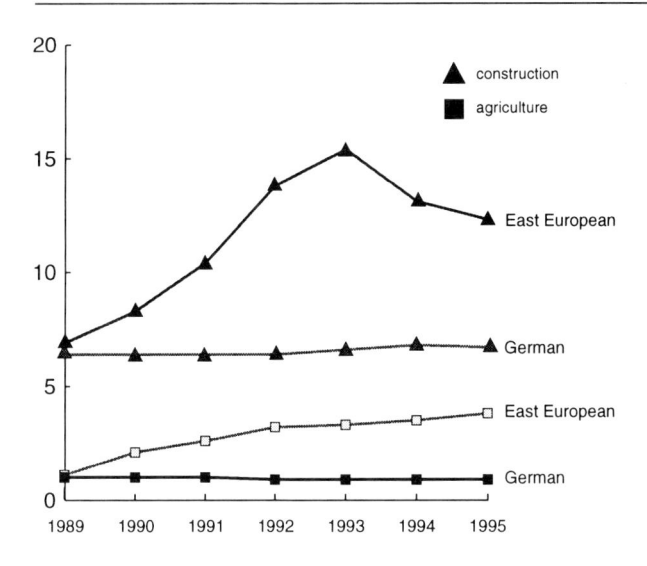

Fig. 6.7: Employment in griculture and construction as a% of total employment, for east Europeans and Germans, 1989–1995

Note: Total employment of Germans (1995) 20,468,050; East Europeans 157,557
Source: Federal Employment Services

have been increasingly concentrated in agriculture and in construction (see Fig. 6.7). There has, however, been some change in the last two years concerning the development of both the absolute figures and shares in total employment.[4]

Looking at the employment of total, German and all foreign employees in agriculture and in construction (Figs. 6.8a and 6.8b overleaf) and comparing this with the development of total unemployment and that of foreigners in these sectors (information on the unemployment of east Europeans is not available), it is interesting to learn that – in contrast to the discussion above – there is no special negative trend until 1995 in these sectors. This effect is even more pronounced if we were to look only at the employment figures for east Europeans.[5] In other words, it is hard to tell a story that the

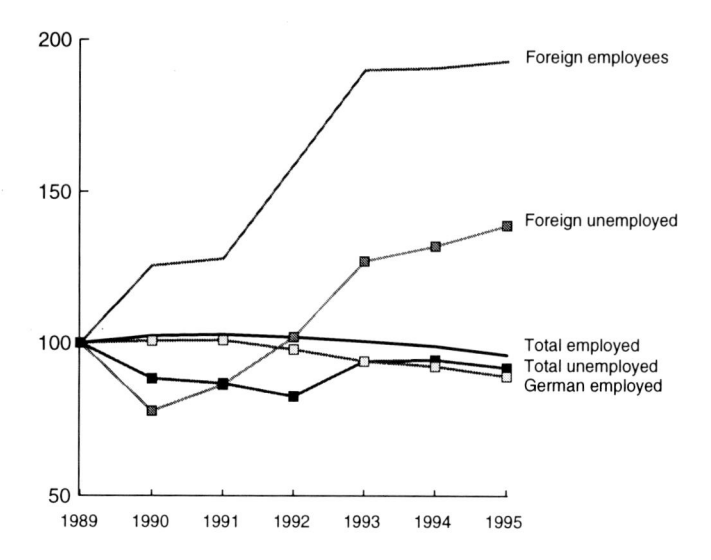

Fig. 6.8a: Agriculture
Index of employment: 1989=100

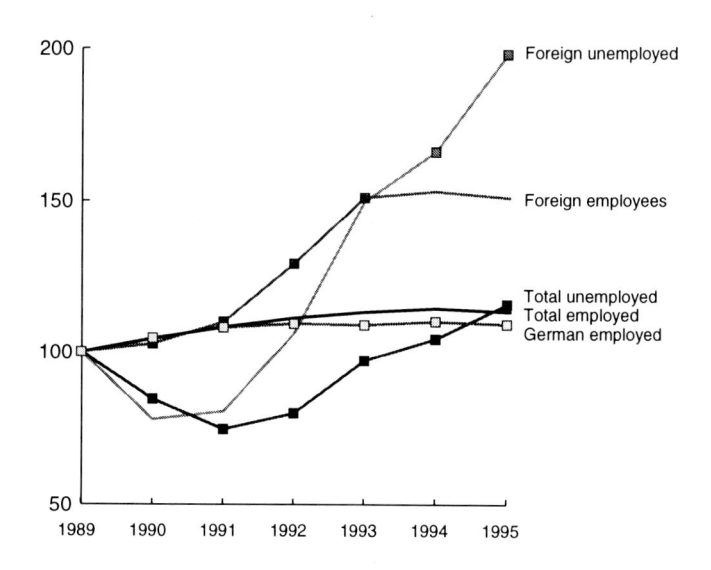

Fig. 6.8b: Construction
Index of employment: 1989=100

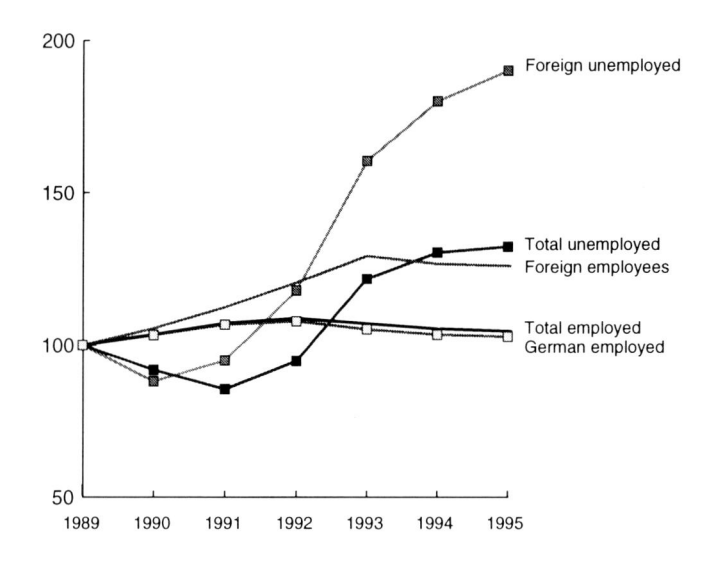

Fig. 6.8c: All branches
Index of employment: 1989=100
Source (Figs. 8a–c): Federal Employment Services
Note: Unemployment figures are for September each year (June for 1995)

employment of east Europeans (and foreigners generally) in these sectors has caused the labour market situation of Germans to be adversely affected. In this respect the apparent correlations for total employment (Fig. 6.8c) may be misleading.

To sum up, there is a clear concentration of legal employment of east Europeans in agriculture and construction. This is partly a result of the official regulations and the admission criteria. But the numbers and shares are not as high as they could negatively influence the resident employment in these branches. In agriculture production would have decreased without the availability of east European workers. But the question is whether it is useful to subsidise a special branch by supplying it with cheap labour from eastern Europe (especially from Poland, with high unemployment in agriculture) instead of opening the market for agricultural goods from this area, and so assisting the economic and labour market development of eastern Europe.

Table 6.8: Estimated Income Transfers of Program Workers to their Home Countries (in thousand DM).

Home Countries	1991	1992	1993	1994	1995	1991–95
Bulgaria	3,533	19,407	40,299	28,181	23,671	115,091
fr. Yugoslavia (total)	162,148	192,157	112,577	88,964	77,848	633,694
among that:						
Rem. Yugoslavia	0	7,349	25,736	145	0	33,231
Bosnia	0	474	12,313	11,345	9,574	33,706
Croatia	0	10,088	63,879	71,109	63,183	208,259
Macedonia	0	0	4,569	6,457	6,892	17,918
Slovenia	0	4,016	19,592	14,837	13,194	51,639
Latvia	0	32	2,677	2,544	1,527	6,780
Poland	503,583	880,457	569,041	496,871	693,342	3,143,294
Romania	17,288	86,020	145,927	35,210	20,628	305,073
fr. Czechoslovakia	130,790	329,622	214,994	157,373	180,989	1,013,769
Slovak Republic	0	0	27,221	34,604	46,103	107,929
Czech Republic	0	0	187,773	122,769	134,886	445,428
Hungary	124,330	172,552	167,994	115,356	116,531	696,763
Total	**941,673**	**1,680,247**	**1,253,508**	**924,500**	**1,114,535**	**5,914,465**

Source: Estimation by the author on the basis of detailed program worker figures and results of surveys on various groups of program workers

Importance of east European employment in Germany for the economy of the home countries

One of the official goals of the work programs for east Europeans in Germany is to provide employment opportunities in Germany, so assisting the east European countries through alleviating their labour market problems and providing income transfers available for economic development. As we have seen the alleviating aspect is not in fact that great. But the other part of the argument seems to be much more important as the following analysis shows.

What are the direct financial effects of the non-permanent employment of east Europeans in Germany. An estimate can be calculated on the basis of the figures available on program workers.[6]

The findings of this estimation (see Table 6.8) are quite surprising. During the five years 1991-1995 the program workers transferred an estimated six billion Deutschmark. Poland alone gained a total income transfer by the program workers of more than three billion DM during this period. Other countries like the Czech Republic, Hungary and Romania also received considerable amounts.

The relevance of these transfers may become obvious with the example of Poland, when comparing it with amounts transferred for foreign direct investment. In 1994, there was a net inflow of foreign direct investment into Poland of about one billion Deutschmark. In the same year, Poland received about DM500 million from income transfers by Polish program workers.

These remittances however, do not mean additional investments of that amount. The crucial point is how the transferred money is used. Information available suggests that migrant workers use the money earned in Germany as follows: a third of the money is spent on consumer goods, another third for re-building, enlarging or newly-building of houses and up to 20 per cent is intended for investments for becoming self-employed (shops, factories or offices). So reasonable parts of the remittances have been used for real investments and for improvement of the housing stock, so directly and positively effecting economic development and the labour market. But the increase in demand for consumer goods will also have positive effects on economic growth and on employment.

Summary and outlook

Immigration from central and eastern Europe reconsidered
Germany has a lot of experience in immigration. But there was no clear immigration policy during that time and a lot of mistakes were made (Martin, 1994). But, concerning the new immigration wave from eastern Europe, it seems that Germany has learnt, at least partly, its lessons. There has been a huge influx from this area to Germany since the end of the last decade. The larger part consists of persons of ethnic German origin and of connected non-German family members. Despite the delicate internal political situation it was possible to stabilise this kind of immigration.

The other part of the influx from eastern Europe has been controlled from the beginning. By introducing programs which provide work opportunities for persons from eastern Europe it was possible to maintain the legal part of these movements and manage them in accordance with the main goals of the programs.

But of course, policy makers are aware of the fact that there is large part of migration pressure where such measures cannot work. There is still a lot of illegal employment in certain sectors and regions, mainly in construction and in some services. The efforts for better control and a reduction of illegal activities have been intensified. The work programmes may have created some opportunities for illegal work. But without those programs the illegal activities would be much more numerous.

Altogether the work programs helped in maintaining control over the migration development and provided legal work opportunities for workers from eastern Europe, for special demand for labour and for limited duration of stay.

Future migration
Migration pressures around the world are increasing. In the short term, income and unemployment differentials in eastern and western Europe are likely to widen, and opinion polls suggest that many eastern Europeans would like to emigrate. But the picture has been changing. Neighbouring eastern countries are themselves becoming immigration countries, partly taking away the immigration pressure on Germany. The main migration pressure is now from the area of the former Soviet Union. Hundreds of thousands of Ukrainians, White Russians and Russians already work legally and illegally in Poland, the Czech Republic and in Hungary. Despite the buffer action of the neighbouring countries, continuing migration from the East must be expected in western Europe, especially in Germany and Austria.

Will western Europe open itself to this migration? From a demographic perspective, it has been suggested that Germany needs immigrants. In Germany, children under 15 are just 15 per cent of the population, and persons 65 and older are also 15 per cent of the population. Without immigration, the German population will decline.

If Germany does not permit immigration, German society and the German economy will have to adjust to fewer consumers – which might be offset by increased exports – and strains on pay-as-you-go social security systems that depend on contributions from workers to support retirees. A shrinking labour force will also have other effects, including effects on

- productivity development
- economic growth

- working hours

- the pensionable age

- duration of military service

- the length of education and training

- the relationship between paid work and family work

- migration policy

There are alternatives to immigration. Lengthening working hours, raising the retirement age, making it easier for women to work and shortening the period of compulsory military service can increase the labour supply. But there are limits to how much additional labour can be gained from such measures. Furthermore, if there are fewer new workforce entrants, then there is a need to train and re-train existing workers to raise productivity, rather than add skills via new work force entrants, and this training reduces hours of work available.

For example, in the former West Germany the labour force will shrink if the participation rate is unchanged and there is no immigration. Of course there are also unemployed workers who could be put to work. There are today more than four million unemployed workers. The fact that immigration has been occurring despite high unemployment suggests that there are structural rigidities such as age, poor health, and lack of qualifications that prevent the unemployed from getting jobs.

Will Germany need immigrants for economic reasons? Probably yes. But it is not possible to predict precisely the additional volume of labour that may be required. For example, if the goal of immigration policy is to maintain the labour force at current levels, then in the year 2000, 200,000 immigrants per year, rising later to higher numbers, would be necessary. This, however is less than recent immigration levels.

What is the conclusion? The need for immigrants is long term. That means that adapting immigration to the short-run situation of the labour market – as the current policy tries to do – makes sense.

Germany needs an immigration policy
Germany has emerged as one of the world's major destinations for immigrants, and immigration pressures are likely to remain high.

Despite decades of immigration, Germany does not consider itself an immigration country. The three immigration goals remain as they were in 1982: a recruitment stop; promoting the integration of legally staying foreigners, above all of the second and third generation; and at the same time, promoting a willingness to return.

There have recently been several new immigration control measures adopted:

- bilateral agreements permit legal entry for employment from Eastern Europe, with the purpose of getting the former illegal streams under legal control and helping economic performance in the sending countries

- a quota was established to limit the number of ethnic Germans from Eastern Europe to 220,000 per year

- there is a recognition of entry rights for family members of persons already staying in Germany

- there are regulations for the distribution of ethnic German immigrants across the regions

- there are some measures concerning assistance for returning migrants and their resettlement in their home country.

These are classic elements of an immigration policy. But they have not been developed consistently. Germany is in the midst of a public discussion of the need for an immigration policy. The outcome of these discussions is likely to be an acknowledgement that Germany is, and is likely to remain, an immigration country. Accepting the inevitability of immigration would permit Germany to discuss

- who and how many should enter

- the effects of immigration on various parts of the German economy and society

- how to struggle against the causes of migration pressure

Germany cannot make or enforce an immigration policy in a vacuum. In co-operation with other rich nations, it will have to work to reduce migration pressure by supporting political stability and economic growth in emigration countries, and perhaps by sharing its wealth with emigration countries.

Endnotes

1. Earlier versions of this paper were prepared for meetings of the Study Group on German-American Migration and Refugee Policies, held in March 1995 in Cambridge, MA, and July 1995 in Ladenburg, Germany.
2. *Übersiedler* are East Germans who emigrated from the former GDR to West Germany. *Aussiedler* are German nationals and people of German origin who emigrated from Central and Eastern Europe to Germany.
3. These are workers officially working on their own account, but in fact under direct instruction of foremen of resident companies. That means that they save contributions to the social insurance and therefore are much cheaper than resident workers. These pseudo-self-employed often come from Great Britain.
4. These graphs are based on official figures. They are not re-calculated in the way we have described in the text. Such a re-calculation would reinforce the impression, since project-tied workers are mainly employed in construction, seasonal workers mainly in agriculture.
5. We have figures for employment of East Europeans by sector (but not employment). These give:

	1989	1990	1991	1992	1993	1994	1995
Agriculture	100	247.8	434.2	752.4	937.9	916.4	980.2
Construction	100	159.0	276.7	524.7	694.8	549.9	515.7
Total	100	132.2	183.7	262.0	312.2	288.8	288.6

    (Source: see Fig. 6.7)
6. These figures have to be combined with the average income per year (related to the average duration of stay) per person in each group. The income is partly estimated by taking usual wages (for project-tied workers, nurses), and there is information from IAB-surveys on border commuters, seasonal workers and of new guest workers. The results have to be reduced by the amount of money spent in Germany (details available in the IAB-surveys).

References

Bauer T & Zimmermann KF (1995) *Integrating the East: The Labour Market Effects of Immigration*, Centre for Economic Policy Research, Discussion Paper Series no. 1235, London.

Chies L & Hönekopp E (1990) "La Germania Occidentale di Fronte a Nuovi Flussi di Lavoro?", *Economia e Lavoro*.

Fassmann H & Münz R (1992) "European East-West Migration 145", *International Migration Review*, vol 28, no. 3/1994.

Gieseck A, Heilemann U & v.Loeffelholz, HD (1994) "Economic Implications of Migration into the Federal Republic of Germany 1988–1992", in *Immigration as an Economic Asset – The German Experience* (Ed. Spencer S), IPPR/Trentham

Gosh B (1994) "The Future of East-West migration", *The Politics of East-West Migration* (Ed. Ardittis S), Houndsmill/London.

Hönekopp E (1991) "Ost-West-Wanderungen: Ursachen und Entwicklung-stendenzen – Bundesrepublik Deutschland und Österreich", in *Mitteilungen aus der Arbeitsmarkt – und Berufsforschung* (MittAB).

Hönekopp E (1992c) "Migratory movements from countries of Central and Eastern Europe – the cases of Germany and Austria", in *People on the move – New migration flows in Europe*, Council of Europe, Strasbourg.

Hönekopp E (1993a) "The Effects of Turkish Accession to the EC on Population and the Labour Market", *Intereconomics*, March/April.

Hönekopp E (1993b) "East-West-Migration: Recent developments concerning Germany, and some future prospects", in *The changing course of international migration*, OECD, Paris.

Hönekopp E (1994) "Germany", in *The Politics of East-West Migration* (Ed. Ardittis S.), London.

Hönekopp E (1995) "The East-West Migration in Europe – Normalization after some Years of Growth", in Heckmann F & Bosswick W, *Migration Policy: A Comparative Perspective*, Stuttgart.

IOM (1993) *Profiles and Motives of Potential Migrants – an IOM study undertaken in four countries: Albania, Bulgaria, Russia and Ukraine*, Geneva.

Hof B (1995) "Zuwanderungsbedarf der Bundesrepublik Deutschland", in *Einwanderungskonzeption für deie Bundesrepublik Deutschland* (Ed. Friedrich-Ebert-Stiftung.), Gesprächskreis Arbeit und Soziales No. 50, Bonn.

Layard R *et al* (1992) *East-West migration: the alternatives*, MIT Press, Cambridge (Mass.)-London

Martin PL (1994) "Germany: Reluctant Land of Immigration", in Cornelius WA, Martin Ph.L. & Hollifield JF, *Controlling Immigration – A Global Perspective*, Stanford.

Öberg S & Wils AB (1992) "East-West Migration in Europe – Can migration theories help estimate the numbers", *POPNET*, vol. 22, Winter.

OECD (1992) *Trends in International Migration*, SOPEMI, Paris.

Polyakov A (1992) *Labour Emigration from the former USSR – Challenges for the European Labour Markets and Cooperation*, paper prepared for the European Labour Market Conference, Glasgow, November.

Straubhaar T (1994) "Ökonomische Bedeutung grenzüberschreitender Arbeitsmigration", in *Europäische Integration und Arbeitsmarkt, Beiträge zur Arbeitsmarkt- und Berufsforschung* (Eds. Weidenfeld W *et al*), vol.181, Nuremberg

Werner H (1995) *Temporary Migration for Employment and Training Purposes and Relevant International Agreements*, Council of Europe, Report to the Select Committee of Experts on Short-Term Migration, Strasbourg.

7. European migration with respect to the Maghreb and Turkey: the social and policy challenge

Donatella Giubilaro

The phenomenon of migration in Europe must be examined in two respects: first, the situation of the immigrant population already living in Europe, and second the potential future influx, and thus the relations between the countries receiving the migrants and their home countries. In this paper the focus is on the Maghreb[1] countries and Turkey, which have been studied within the current IBO research programme into migratory pressures.

The issue of migration into the EU must be seen in its European political context. It is from the moment that the countries affected realised that they could no longer control the phenomenon of migration, that migration became a real political challenge, and came to be considered one of the most important socio-economic questions of today. It is also from this moment that the concept of migratory pressure was developed.

Efforts are currently being made to establish an effective system to control the arrival in Europe of immigrants from developing countries. But the current political crisis in this matter makes fresh evaluation essential. The countries of Europe are beginning to realise that while a less timid common policy in the matter of immigration and political asylum is essential, it is insufficient. It must be accompanied by measures dealing with the underlying factors which influence immigration. It is important therefore that European policy-makers take into account the views of the countries from where immigrants come, and of their long-term interests which are largely determined by their development needs.

The flow of immigration

We must make a distinction between countries having a long-term tradition of immigration and those of southern Europe who have only been recently confronted by this phenomenon. We can say that in general the labour market in the European countries requires immigrant labour which is more adapted to their needs, better qualified or more mobile than the internal labour force, or for the immigrant workers to be already legally settled. On the one hand it is to be noted that it is almost exclusively workers with skills in demand who compose the new flow of authorised worker immigration. On the other hand, unauthorised and seasonal workers seem better able to fulfil the need for mobility, which coincides with the development of small firms, and thus meet current needs in the agricultural and construction sectors.

From the 1960s to the mid-1970s, the Maghreb and Turkish immigrants entering Europe were young unskilled workers, fulfilling the labour needs of European industries. Such workers undertook hard, badly paid work which was unacceptable to the indigenous labour force and even to well-established immigrants. This flow of fresh labour went to France, Germany, Belgium, The Netherlands and Sweden, and was controlled by agreements between the countries of origin and those receiving the immigrants.

Following the closure of frontiers in 1973–74, immigration was restricted to the families of workers entering under family reunification auspices as well as a small number of highly qualified workers (See Fig. 7.1 – for the example of France). In fact in these countries the closing of frontiers was to some extent an illusion. Most steady inflows cannot be reduced because they are legally based on the fundamental right to family life. At least in part the remaining inflows, both legal and illegal, can also be considered as irreducible, since they are a solution to the shortage of workers in some sectors of the European labour market.

The flows of immigration, above all of Moroccans towards Spain, and Moroccans and Tunisians towards Italy, began at the start of the 1980s. This was partly the result of the stopping of immigration into countries traditionally allowing it, and partly of the demands of companies engaged in subcontracting and the informal economy, seeking workers who would accept low pay and "flexible" working conditions. To start with, immigration was encouraged by the absence of legal controls over entry and residence. Once this trend had started, it tended to be self-perpetuating, being fed by immigrant networks. Now that regulations exist, and that frontier controls have become more effective, the numbers of immigrants seem to have stabilised. Nevertheless there remains the problem of illegal immigration. Up to now flows have consisted of individual young unqualified workers, but family reunifications are already under way, notably amongst the Moroccan immigrants in Italy, and will require an

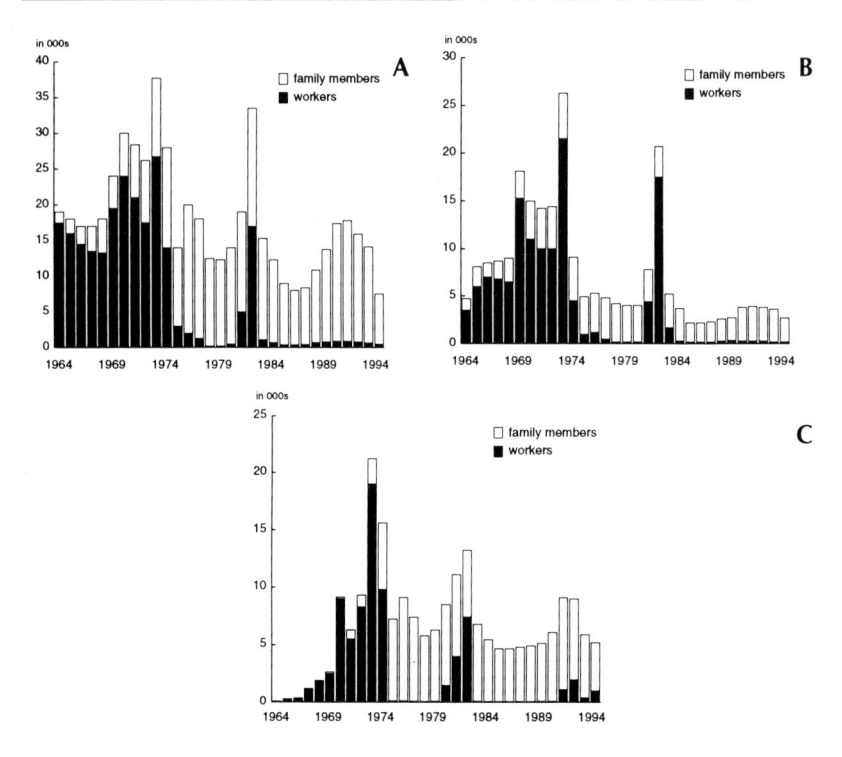

Graph 7.1: France immigration flows
A: Moroccan B: Tunisian C: Turkish

adequate policy response. However, since 1990 the scale of family reunification flows from the Maghreb countries entering France, the Netherlands and Belgium have decreased or stabilised compared with previous inflows. If this phenomenon is confirmed in the coming years, it will mean that family reunification is losing its importance.[2]

If the current rates of immigration seem to be decreasing, the potential rate of immigration will continue to be considerable, given the high pressure to emigrate inside the countries of origin. This is mainly due to the inability of the employment markets in Turkey and Maghreb countries to create sufficient jobs to satisfy the increasing numbers of those seeking employment, as young people reach working age (see Fig. 7.2).

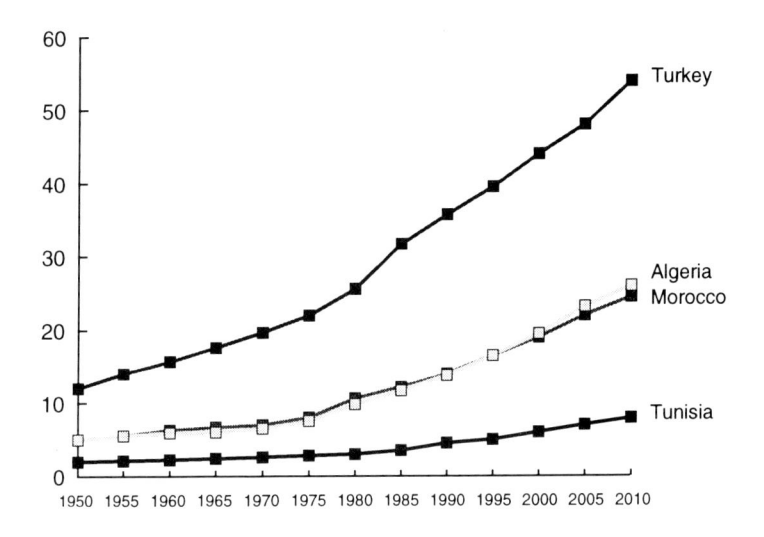

Graph 7.2: Working age population
millions
Source: data from UN (1994 revision). After 1995 these are forecasts.

The size of foreign populations in Europe

For Europe as a whole the classification of foreign populations (non-EU) by country of origin shows us that the Turkish population is the largest, ahead of the Maghreb community (see Figs. 7.3 & 7.4 overleaf). The fact that Turkish immigrants take first place, and that Germany has the highest number of resident immigrants in the European Economic Area, (3,698 millions in 1990) ahead of France (2,273 million in 1990), results not merely from past inflows of immigrants, but also from the special features of German nationality law.

The phenomenon of the growth in the number of immigrants has two explanations (depending on when it started). In countries with long-term immigration, the growth in the number of immigrants from 1973–74 onwards is due to family regrouping (see Fig. 7.1), as well as the consequential natural growth of the population. We can for instance observe that the principle factor in France affecting the increase in its alien population is natural growth: immigrant women from the Maghreb have a

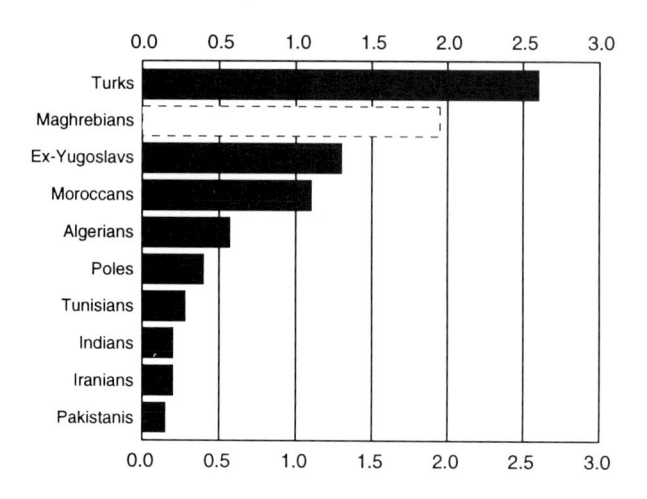

Fig. 7.3: Main groups of developing country nationals residing in EEA (as at 1 January 1992)
(millions)

Source: OECD, Eurostat (Figs. 7.3 and 7.4)

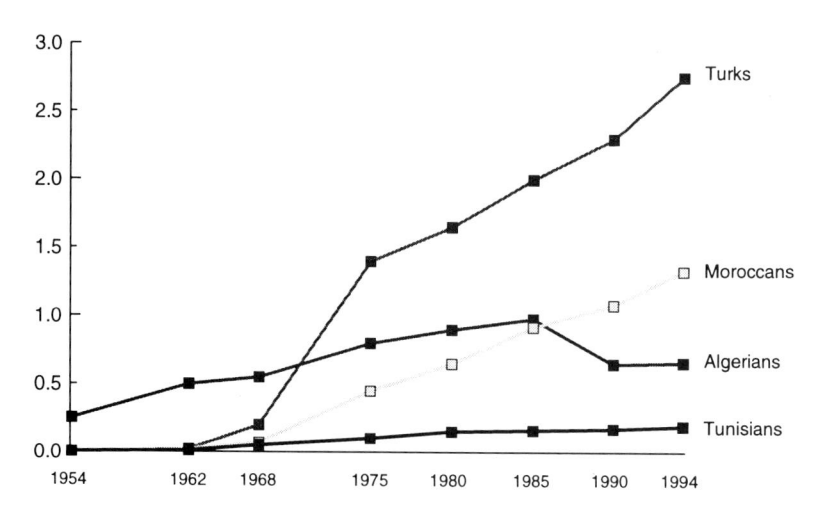

Fig. 7.4: Evolution of Turkey and Maghreb nationals residing in EEA
(millions)

higher fertility rate than French women. As a result the percentage of immigrants in the total population has increased solely because of this natural growth. Nevertheless the fertility rate in the second generation of immigrant women seems to be approximate to France's national average.

In a fairly short space of time the numbers of foreign residents in Italy and Spain have reached high levels, especially after the "regularisations" of controls in 1985-86 and 1991 in Spain, and in 1986-87 and 1990-91 in Italy[3]. In Spain the number of Moroccan residents, estimated at 5,200 in 1985, now stands at 61,000. In Italy the number of Tunisians, estimated at 4,400 in 1985, had grown to over 50,000 in 1993, while the Moroccans, some 2,600 in 1985 had increased to over 97,000 in 1994. However, the number of Tunisians declined in Italy in 1994, as did that of Moroccans in 1995.This suggests that inflows have been reduced during the last years compared with the past. Nevertheless a judgement on the development of the situation will be possible only once the current regularisation is finished. Only at that stage we will have new data that will take into account illegal inflows that have taken place in recent years.

As far as policy towards immigrants is concerned, in countries with a tradition of immigration, there are examples of policies of assimilation (France), integration (Belgium and Germany) and multi-culturalism (The Netherlands). In Italy and in Spain the large number of immigrants and the admission of their families will oblige their governments to put a suitable policy into effect. If such a policy is not implemented, there will be instability which could lead to xenophobic reactions, and signs of social friction which could be aggravated by the appearance of a second generation of immigrants. Italy apparently tends towards a policy of multi-culturism. But will there be the political will at both national and regional levels to provide the financial means for such action?

Current political challenges concerning the immigrant population established in Europe

A common social and economic policy concerning the immigrants living in the territory of member countries has yet to appear at European Union level. It is to be hoped that member countries will at least agree a system to co-ordinate their existing policies. Harmonising these policies would allow, among other matters, the free movement of workers within the Union to become a reality.

Matters which could enter this co-ordination framework would include measures aimed at fighting unemployment among immigrants, as well as racial discrimination against migrant workers in the employment market. Specific programmes could also be created to integrate new immigrants, including women, as well as second or third generation immigrants (who often have never migrated themselves). Such programmes could offer courses in languages as well as technical training.

Attacking discrimination against immigrant workers and workers from ethnic minorities in the labour market is one of the most important methods of guaranteeing the integration of such populations. A specific non-discrimination programme for such workers is organised by the International Labour Organisation (ILO) in 11 countries, including 8 members of the EU (Germany, Belgium, Denmark, Spain, Finland, The Netherlands, United Kingdom and Sweden). The objective of this programme is to support governments, as well as worker and employer organisations, in the fight against discrimination in the labour market, which persists despite it being forbidden by law. It would seem desirable to create such a programme for all EU countries. It would then be possible, by comparing the different methods used by member countries and their effectiveness, to attempt to understand the best methods of fighting practices which are both morally unacceptable and economically wasteful. In addition, such actions could support a European programme aimed at the successful cohabitation of immigrant populations with those of the host countries. The results of such a programme covering the whole of the EU could also be the basis for formulating a European directive aimed at fighting discrimination against immigrant workers.

Current challenges in EU foreign policy

It is said that as a matter of policy, both the EU and the Maghreb must jointly handle the question of migration, but this aim has up to now remained more theoretical than practical. The bilateral agreements in the 1970s between Turkey and the Maghreb countries on the one hand and the European Community on the other, foresaw social measures to establish non-discrimination in working conditions, pay and social security benefits of migrants from these countries in any member-nation of the Community. These agreements have remained dormant, given that the bilateral agreements with EC countries which controlled Maghreb and Turkish immigration were considered to be more advantageous by the countries of origin. Nevertheless the European Court of Justice has taken account of these measures in several of its judgements.

In the last few years, particularly during the preliminary discussions on new EU-Maghreb agreements, it has been the hope that policies such as collaboration for development, trade liberalisation and incentives for private investment could be regarded as an alternative to migration.

The first series of co-operation agreements were signed in 1976 between the European Community and Tunisia, Morocco and Algeria. The new association agreements signed in 1995 between the EU and Tunisia, and the EU and Morocco, include provisions concerning migrant workers which are no different from previous treaties. Nevertheless these agreements attempt, even if somewhat timidly, to go beyond existing policies concerning workers in Europe, by addressing questions relating to the development of their countries of origin.

Co-operation for development
To consolidate social co-operation the new agreements have given priority to measures aimed at reducing migratory pressure, notably through programmes for creating employment and developing vocational training in emigration areas, as well as reinstating repatriates returned because of their illegal status in the Economic Union.

This seems to indicate rising awareness of the fact that the two sides will be drawn into collaborating not only on long-term development programmes tackling potential migration, but also programmes for restructuring the labour market, and for job creation, which rapidly impact on the trend to emigration.

Into this framework also comes the initiative on the Maghreb Programme launched under the auspices of the ILO with financial backing from Italy. This brought together those responsible from the three Maghreb states, as well as representatives of the main European countries engaged in bilateral co-operation with them, so as to encourage them to collaborate within a programme aimed at making use of public development funds to speed up the creation of new employment and on wealth, so as to reduce progressively the need to emigrate for economic reasons. Unfortunately, analysis and talk has not been followed up at the level of international co-operation. Nevertheless, within the framework of the Maghreb Programme, Italian co-operation has financed a programme for Morocco and Tunisia, which could be regarded as a pilot scheme, set up by the ILO, promoting very small businesses and improving job training.

Trade liberalisation
The new agreements postulate the creation of a free trade area. The external trade of the Maghreb countries is very largely with Europe. For this reason, within the framework of programmes for structural adjustment and economic growth, free trade agreements with the countries of the EU are seen as essential for the countries of the Maghreb, so as to allow them to enter the world trading system.

A free trade zone should be established progressively over a period of twelve years. The new agreements confirm the preferential treatment currently given by the Community to products from Turkey and the Maghreb countries, and in practice open fully the European markets to Maghreb exports of industrial products and make concessions on the bulk of farm exports. An improvement in this regime is foreseen for farm and fishing products, concerning quotas for duty-free imports and the levels of duty payable above such quota limits.

With the gradual bringing into effect of these agreements, Maghreb businesses will be able to enjoy to the full their comparative advantages thanks to lower labour costs. The Maghreb countries will thus have the incentive to specialise in labour intensive areas like manufacturing and food industries, and to increase exports to the EU market, which is protected against similar imports from elsewhere.

While these agreements, and the close proximity of their markets should encourage the expansion of production in Turkey and the Maghreb countries, and even the relocation of European companies to these areas, the competition from east European and Asiatic production must not be underestimated. In fact the EU markets will also gradually be opened up to imports from eastern Europe, thanks to preferential agreements, as well as to imports from Asia, as a result of bringing the GATT agreements into effect. Further, in the very sensitive sector of textiles, and with the ending of the multi-fibre agreement, the Maghreb countries will loose their privileged position in comparison with other regions. Competition in this sector is strong, given that in some other areas, production costs are often lower than those of Turkey or the Maghreb countries. Companies in these last-mentioned areas can only expand their exports and attract direct foreign investment if they improve their productivity and marketing, and the countries must maintain a particularly favourable political and economic climate.

Within the framework of the free trade agreements, the liberalisation of fresh trade will be reciprocal. Because of this, the Maghreb countries which up to now have given no concessions to the Community, will progressively eliminate the obstacles to the import of EU manufactured goods, and grant it preferential rights for the import of agricultural products. Beyond the loss of tax revenue, the coming into effect of these measures will oblige existing Maghreb companies to endure the competition of European imports.

In the short term, free trade could give rise to the growth of imports into the Maghreb, the deterioration of its balance of trade, the imposition of additional measures to limit public expenditure, a lowering of the standard of living, and in consequence an increase in the pressure to migrate. Despite these negative effects, the opening up of the Maghreb markets to European companies is nevertheless one of the steps necessary to encourage foreign investment. Only in the long term, if the creation of a free trade area succeeds in attracting investment, and favours continued economic expansion, can such an area be seen as offering alternatives to emigration.

However, no free trade agreement with the Maghreb or customs union with Turkey will ever go as far as to foresee the free movement of people between the EU and other Mediterranean countries.

The question which now arises is the duration of likely harmful effects of the opening up of trade, and how to guarantee that as a second stage there will be an economic lift-off, able to create sufficient employment to satisfy each country's needs. The whole process depends upon there being a sufficiently favourable climate to attract foreign investment, and the relocation of European companies. Targeted steps in co-operation or trade liberalisation can only be considered as accompanying measures in support of investment projects which must be created by private industry, and they must not be regarded as the substitute for such projects.

Political Dialogue
The European Union is aware of the fact that the international challenge of migration from now on requires consideration within a wider political and economic perspective. Within the Euro-Mediterranean agreements, there must be a regular political exchange of views between the parties, aimed at the stability and security of the Mediterranean region. Such a dialogue envisages regular bilateral meetings to discuss international questions of mutual interest. Immigration matters should be dealt with within such an arrangement.

Given the strategic importance of the Mediterranean, the project for creating a Euro-Mediterranean Partnership in 2010, for which an initial conference was held in Barcelona in November 1995, is very important. All the agreements signed until now are considered by the EU as bilateral agreements because they involve only one foreign country at the time. The Euro-Mediterranean partnership would represent a change in this situation, at least at the political level because it would represent the first multilateral agreement with all the Mediterranean partners: Morocco, Algeria, Tunisia, Egypt, Syria, Jordan, Lebanon, Palestine, Israel, Turkey, Malta and Cyprus. It thus aims to strengthen relationships in this region through a global and co-ordinated approach, and be an addition to the strengthening of bilateral relations. The questions of migration itself, and in particular of migratory pressure, of the integration of migrants and of illegal migration will be treated together as priority matters within the three dimensions, political, economic and socio-cultural, that constitute this partnership.

The role of local level actors

Local level agents (or "actors") must guarantee a policy of integration for resident immigrant populations and, in some cases achieve this even in the absence of regulations or support at national level. Even local level actors should be interested in collaborating at European level, as well as with their opposite numbers in the countries which the emigrants have left behind, to exchange experiences and to ensure the success of their policies.

In the countries that the migrants have left, and within the framework of parallel measures to encourage the development of labour-intensive industries, thanks to foreign investment, actors in the field also have a role to play. These actors can contribute both independently and in programmes of decentralised co-operation, to encourage on the one hand the countries of the Maghreb to attract foreign investment, and on the other to support the efforts of European entrepreneurs who want to invest in the Maghreb, or to set up decentralised production there, but who are finding it difficult to do so. Such contributions can occur because it is at the decentralised level in Europe and in partnership with their opposite numbers in other countries that they will put to good use the already existing experience and knowledge which is required to understand the needs of industrialists and the potential offered by the Maghreb and Turkey.

For example, co-operation between local authorities could aim at the creation of an administrative environment adapted to attract and receive foreign investment, or chambers of commerce could provide the liaison between the needs expressed by European companies wanting to invest abroad and the target countries. Training organisations could concentrate on the needs for training in such areas as management, productivity and quality control. Based on national expertise in Europe, know-how in the development of small-scale industries, and sub-contracting, could be supplied. Within this framework the regional programmes of decentralised co-operation already set up by the European Community can also operate fruitfully.[4]

The objective of this undertaking at a decentralised level would not only be long-term action for the development of Turkey and the Maghreb countries, but also support for measures to reduce the migratory pressure, and political security in the Mediterranean. For actors in the field the objective would also be to become involved in the world-wide spread of knowledge and experience. And the aim will further be to guarantee that economic development, European investment and the relocation of European companies will have positive effects in the European countries, and will not merely result in the loss of jobs, or the absence of any creation of new employment.

Endnotes

1. The Maghreb countries are Tunisia, Algeria and Morocco.
2. An analysis of inflows can be done only for France, the Netherlands, Germany and Belgium. For Spain and Italy, inflow data are not available and all studies are based on foreign populations residing in the country.
3. Governments have from time to time found it necessary to call an amnesty allowing illegal immigrants to declare themselves to regularise their status. Regularisation laws establish terms and conditions to which illegal immigrants have to correspond in order to obtain the regularisation. If they do so they become defined as foreign population legally residing in the country and so the official statistics always show an increase in the scale of foreign population residing in the country.
4. In 1992 the European community approved "the Renewed Mediterranean Policy". This new co-operation policy has taken place in parallel to the traditional co-operation activities that consisted of projects financed by the EU and implemented in each developing country of the Mediterranean region. The characteristics of the Renewed Mediterranean Policy are the decentralisation and the regionalisation of projects financed. Decentralisation, because the realisation of this new co-operation has implied the active participation of bodies such as universities, the media, municipalities and enterprises. Regionalisation, because projects have involved participants of several countries, both Mediterranean non-member countries and EU countries. Within this framework several programmes exist: MED-URBS between local authorities, MED-CAMPUS between universities, MED-INVEST between enterprises, MED-MEDIA between media, MED-MIGRATION between local authorities and associations for migration matter. The aims of these programmes are to have representatives of civil societies working together on subjects of common interest and to have an exchange of experiences.

Other IPPR reports:

Strangers and Citizens
edited by Sarah Spencer
Mar 1994 £14.95 1 85489 051 4
Recommends a more infomred, rational and principled approach to British immigration, refugees and citizenship policies which would meet the UK's international human rights obligations, reflect the economic demand for selective immigration and improve race relations.

Immigration as an economic asset: the German experience
edited by Sarah Spencer
May 1994 £10.95 1 85856 010 1
Argues that European governments could allay some concern about immigration if they told the public about the economic benefits which immigrants bring. Here, German economists and social scientists present research findings which show the positive contribution that immigrants have made to the German economy.

European Union Citizenship
Síofra O'Leary
June 1996 £9.95 1 86030 037 5
The form of citizenship agreed at Maastricht is an ill-conceived and badly executed attempt to conceal rather than address the real democratic difficulties which face the EU.

Social Democracy at the Heart of Europe
Donald Sassoon
July 1996 £7.50 1 86030 040 5
European integration has so far been driven by economics. The completion of the single market means that this has been achieved. The transformation of the EU into a "People's Europe" is a different goal – one which can only be addressed by a European Charter. Sassoon presents his argument clearly and persuasively.

Transformation and Integration:
Shaping the future of eastern and central Europe
by J Eatwell et al
October 1995 £12.95 1 86030 011 1
A report which goes beyond the arid debate over "shock therapy" and "gradualism" and faces the question of what can be done next for the economies of central and eastern Europe. Argues that the future prosperity and security of Europe depends on devising policies which transform the former Communist states into socially just and environmentally sustainable economies.

All these reports and many others are available from IPPR, 30–32 Southampton Street, London WC2E 7RA tel: 0171-470 6100